FREDRIK FRANSON

FREDRIK FRANSON

A Model for
Worldwide Evangelism

by Edvard P. Torjesen

William Carey Library

Pasadena, California 91104

Library of Congress Cataloging in Publication Data

Torjesen, Edvard P., 1924-
  Fredrik Franson, model for worldwide frontier evangelism.

  1. Franson, Fredrik, 1852-1908.   2. Missionaries—Biography.
3. Evangelists—Biography. I. Title. BV3705.F7T67 1982
266'.0092'4 [B] 82-17892
ISBN 0-87808-191-7

International Standard Book Number 0-87808-191-7

Published by the William Carey Library
P.O. Box 40129
Pasadena, California 91104
Telephone (213) 798-0819

Cover: Graphics by Gene Keller. Fredrik Franson portrait by
Warner Sallman.

PRINTED IN THE UNITED STATES OF AMERICA

CONTENTS

In Search of a Church Model-15
Fredrik Franson's Conversion and Early Development-17
The Interdenominational Evangelist-18
Two Principles of the New Testament Church-20
An Unexpected Application in Utah-21
A Free Evangelical Church in Denver-23
Fruit in Nebraska: Four New Congregations-25
Some of Franson's Statements on Biblical Church Polity-26
Toward the Any Moment Expectation of Christ's Return-28
The Founding of the Evangelical Free Church of America-30

The First Eight Months in Sweden-34
The Karlstad Example-35
Persecution Unleashed-37
Franson's Response-39
A Visit to England-40
The Norway Campaign-41
The Background-42
Franson's Parting Counsel and the Founding of the Mission
  Covenant of Norway-45

Contents

ACKNOWLEDGMENT

The following material first appeared as a paper, "Fredrik Franson After 100 Years," prepared for the Consultation of Organizations with a Franson Heritage, held at Jönköping, Sweden, May 27–30, 1981.

I wish to acknowledge and thank Dr. Vernon Mortenson, former General Director of TEAM and now Chairman of its Board of Directors, for his great personal encouragement and help in editing this material for wider presentation. My prayer is that God may use and bless this presentation to inspire and awaken in all of us something of the spirit of Fredrik Franson. Then we too may be able to mobilize ourselves for effective communication of the Gospel to people in societies all around the earth, and like Franson, with expectancy "look forward to the day of God and speed its coming" (II Peter 3:12 NIV).

The Author

viii

FOREWORD

Years of study and research have brought together a mountain of material in almost a dozen languages on the life and work of Fredrik Franson. That which is presented here is an overview of that material. This striking model of evangelism and church planting, beginning in the 19th century and stretching into the 20th, has much to teach us as we approach the 21st. Until our Lord returns we must carry on this vital work of world evangelization and the beginning and development of churches. Fredrik Franson provides us with invaluable help through both precept and example.

We owe a great debt to the researcher of this outstanding missionary, evangelist, and churchman—Fredrik Franson. The researcher, Ed Torjesen, a TEAM missionary, was originally assigned to Mongolia. He also served in Taiwan among the Amis tribespeople and Chinese Mainlanders. The son of European missionaries who served in China, Torjesen is familiar with the languages and cultures of Asia, Europe, and North America. He is thus well equipped to trace the ministry and writings of Franson on several continents. His research has taken him to many countries in Europe and North America, with correspondence from as far afield as

New Zealand, South Africa, and Brazil. He has drawn from many scores of sources, including university libraries, church archives, state and national museums, libraries, and many individuals.

It is our prayer that many will read this material and will look forward to future publications for all that they will have to teach us about this remarkable individual so blessed of God and used so mightly in so many parts of the world.

Richard Winchell, General Director
The Evangelical Alliance Mission

INTRODUCTION

Fredrik Franson probably did not expect to be memorialized for his work. Nothing has been found in all the extensive research on his life and work to indicate that he ever did one thing designed to perpetuate his own memory. If others made such suggestions he must have vetoed them promptly. His eagerness for the return of Christ and his expectation of Ilis soon return would have made him consider a memorial as having little meaning. After all, there would not be any of the Lord's children around to take note of a memorial!

Franson, however, did leave a significant memorial—almost anonymously! He won uncounted thousands of souls to the Lord. He founded churches, often from the converts of a single campaign. He laid down guidelines for church fellowships. He founded, guided, and promoted missionary societies which have an ongoing history of effective ministry. These organizations, which do not bear his name in any way, are indeed memorials to a most remarkable servant of the Lord.

The ministry of Franson began in 1874 on a very low key and by 1877 had reached a high level of intensity and fruitfulness that continued unabated to 1908 the year of his early death.

This is now the twentieth century, and almost three quarters of a century have passed since Franson's death. The question may be asked, "What did this man, so little known to general church and mission history, do to merit attention now?" A better question might be, "What biblical principles of vision, action, and organization did he exemplify and propound that gave stability and permanence to his work and should have continual emphasis now?"

Libraries and archives in many countries contain much material on the work of Fredrik Franson recorded at the time of his active ministry, but most of that material is in languages other than English and thus has remained unresearched by the English-speaking church and mission historians. For those who work in the Scandinavian languages and German the research has been more fruitful and rewarding. Several other languages—French, Spanish, Afrikaans, among them—are not without their records.

This presentation is a condensation of material which properly should—and some day may—be published in several volumes. These historical facts relate primarily to the principles in Franson's ministry that he built into seven mission societies he founded and the other organizations which recognize his early and yet decisive influence.

Fredrik Franson was born in Sweden June 17, 1852, emigrated to the United States in 1869, was converted in 1872, was motivated by the Lord to begin serving Him in 1874, began public evangelistic campaigns in 1877, and became widely known among Scandinavians through his evangelism and writing. He helped organize the second premillennial conference on record in the United States in 1881.

From 1881 to 1890 he ministered extensively in Sweden, Norway, Denmark, Finland, Germany, Switzerland, France, Italy, the Near East, and Russia. He was in the United States during the periods 1890-92, 1896-97, 1901-2. The rest of his time from 1890 to 1908 was spent in Europe, on the different fields of the world to which his missionaries had gone, and in many other countries as well. Of him it could be said as of the apostles, "And they went forth, and preached everywhere, the Lord working with them" (Mark 16:20).

Vernon Mortenson

1

FREDRIK FRANSON AND CHURCH DEVELOPMENT ON THE AMERICAN FRONTIER

During the decade which we have just entered, several of the organizations founded by Fredrik Franson will be celebrating their 100th anniversary. However, four local churches founded through Franson's early evangelistic ministry already in 1980 celebrated their 100th anniversary. Fredrik Franson was a church founder before he was a missions founder. In a very complicated and frustrating cross-cultural situation, in which the Swedish Lutheran pietist settlers on the American frontier still had not been able to formulate and apply a satisfactory concept of the church, Franson helped them develop a concept that was both culturally viable and biblically sound. It became one of the guiding concepts in the emergence of the Evangelical Free Church of America a few years later.

How did the young Franson get into such a church founding and church development ministry? Let us take a look at the setting, the Swedish-American spiritual awakening, and Franson's own development within that awakening.

In Search of a Church Model

When the Swedish Lutheran pietists—"readers" as they were called—first began settling on the American frontier, they faced a serious problem. They had no Swedish Lutheran model of the church which they could apply in their new frontier environment. It was 1850 before the first local Swedish Lutheran church could be organized among them, and then that was done under the auspices of the American Congregational Home Missionary Society. However, by then the Methodists already were several years ahead in their efforts to found churches among the Swedish immigrants. By 1852 the Baptists also had started their work. But in 1851 the Swedish Lutherans did join with other Lutherans in organizing the Synod of Northern Illinois. Then the Swedish Lutheran pietists became disenchanted, because this synod would not adopt the "unaltered" Augsburg Confession but affirmed only that this Confession was "mainly correct." In 1860 they organized the Scandinavian Evangelical Augustana Synod which did then adopt the "unaltered" Augsburg Confession.

When immigration began to increase after 1865, and large numbers of people touched by the revivals in Sweden began arriving, these people discovered little appreciation within the Augustana Synod for the emphasis on "the new life in Christ," which had been the unifying theme of the revivals in Sweden. Nevertheless, the revival did spread within these Augustana churches, but with it, tensions also arose. In 1868, which was one year before Fredrik Franson arrived in the United States, pietists in one of the Northern Illinois Synod churches and in two of the Augustana Synod churches organized themselves as local Lutheran missionary associations.[1] The latter two used the Jönköping Missionary Association in Sweden, now merged with the Swedish Alliance Mission, as their model. Through this process the Swedish Lutheran revival people on the American frontier soon began discovering each other. Missionary associations sprang up in many places. It was a time of great blessing. Soon, however, it became clear that more was needed than missionary associations. Church nurture

---

[1] As used in this paper, "missionary association" refers to groups for Christian fellowship and evangelistic witness which were not formally organized as churches.

was needed. This they tried to provide through the associations. But again more was needed. In 1873 they called a meeting and organized the Swedish Evangelical Lutheran Mission Synod. However, a schism took place, and in 1874 the Synod of Ansgar also was organized.

Fredrik Franson's Conversion and Early Development

It was during these developments on the Swedish-American frontier that in 1872 the 20-year-old Fredrik Franson found the Lord in his frontier home at Estina, Nebraska. He had been sickly and depressed since his first winter on the frontier. Now with his conversion he began an intensive study of God's Word and current Christian thinking, but he apparently never shared his faith with anyone except his mother. Two years later a revival broke out in the Estina Baptist Church, the only church in their little settlement in eastern Nebraska. An older lady came to deal with the still timid and withdrawn young man. God convicted him of his negligence in not publicly confessing Christ. He then dedicated himself fully to the Lord and began immediately to witness. Soon he and his parents were baptized. He became an active Baptist layman. In 1875 the young Fredrik Franson was elected secretary of the Scandinavian Baptist Conference of Nebraska, Western Iowa, and Dakota.

That fall, however, Franson began another significant period of study and development. Though no primary sources on him during this period have been found, secondary sources suggest that he went to the East Coast where, from October 1875 until April 1876, he probably studied and worked in D. L. Moody's campaigns in Brooklyn, Philadelphia, and Manhattan. He may have even stayed there until August. In time, however, he left for Chicago where it is certain that he worked in and studied D. L. Moody's great Chicago campaign from October 1876 till January 1877.

During this period Franson had encountered the heart pulse of the Anglo-American revival movement. He had carefully observed interdenominational cooperation on an evangelical basis. He had discovered the biblical basis and method of aggressive evangelism. He had also become thoroughly familiar with the issues involved in the various Anglo-American and German-American discussions and expositions of premillennial eschatology. To the perspectives of the Swedish-American spiritual awakening Franson now added the perspectives of the Anglo-American and German-American spiritual awakenings. He developed his own case for the biblical necessity of the premillennial interpretation and the any-moment-expectancy of Christ's return.[2]

The Interdenominational Evangelist

In February 1877 Franson, at 24½ years of age, began his first public campaign as an interdenominational evangelist at Swede Bend, Iowa. Fifty-four years later Miss Minnie Lund, the local school teacher and organist, penned this eyewitness account:

> The greatest revival ever witnessed here was conducted by evangelist Fredrik Franson who came as an undenominational missionary sent out by the Samson Mission of New York [sic]. . . . Crowds to overflowing gathered at both churches. Even standing room was at a premium. Nevertheless, people flocked in from all directions. Many of them walked several miles through swamps and thickets but none could stay home in the midst of such outpouring of God's spirit.
>
> The evangelist also brought a singer which added to the interest. Good singing was such a treat, and he surely sang the Gospel into the hearts of the listeners. He also led the audience to sing—and such singing those people did! At both morning and evening services one would think the heavenly hosts had come again to visit the earth as they did at Bethlehem on that first Christmas morning.
>
> These special revival meetings were held in February 1877 and continued for several weeks. There were many additions to both churches as a result.

For the next two and a half years Franson was busy with evangelistic campaigns in various places in Minnesota,

---

[2] The use of "any-moment-expectancy" rather than "imminent" in this paper is for the purpose of more adequately conveying Franson's conviction that Christ could indeed, and not merely as a matter of abstract doctrine, return at any moment.

Iowa, and Nebraska. He worked in churched and un-churched settlements. He worked in Mission Synod, Synod of Ansgar, and Baptist churches. The Augustana research-er John Olson Anders reported about his Minnesota cam-paigns:

> Franson was moved to preach in churches of all denominations. The Lutherans opposed his activity, but both Baptists and Missions Friends welcomed him. His camp meetings at Stanchfield occasioned great revivals. "This spiritual awakening continued with more or less power throughout the state for a number of years. At times it seemed to have finished its course, when all at once it would start anew." In August 1878 August Bryngelsen joined Fran-son at Wyanette which he made the center of extensive itinerant activity. These activities resulted in the organiza-tion of a number of mission congregations before the end of 1884.

Another co-worker with whom Franson teamed up at some time during this period was John F. Fredrickson, the St. Paul man who later was to be associated with him both in Utah and in the Himalayas.

On August 4, 1878, Fredrik Franson was received into the membership of the Moody Church in Chicago. On that same day he also was given a letter from the Executive Committee of the church with the following commendation: "The bear-er, Rev. F. Franson, having won our confidence during the time he has been among us (he being a member of our church) and going forth now in evangelistic work, we com-mend him to the Lord and to the Lord's people wherever his labors call him." Franson must therefore also have spent some time in Chicago before this date.

It is not clear why he transferred his church membership from the Estina Baptist Church to the Moody Church but some matter of conviction surely was involved. He took a clear and definite initiative to be identified with this evangelistic, interdenominational, independent local church. We may assume that it was in order to better carry out the evangelistic work to which he now felt God was call-ing him. He needed to be in a church that was not only culturally viable and biblical, but also one from which he could serve in all segments of the Swedish-American revival movement with a minimum of difficulty.

Two Principles of the New Testament Church

Clearly Fredrik Franson was deeply concerned about the unstable and fragmented church situation in the Swedish-American revival movement. His earliest extant article appeared on May 23, 1879. It was entitled (in English translation), "A Contribution to the Solution of the Complicated Denominational and Local Church Question." It was an effort to show "a good way to take" out of the problems that had arisen due to the denominational fragmentation of the revival movement, not the least of which was through the continuation of the two pietist Lutheran synods, the Mission Synod and the Synod of Ansgar. The article shows also that even at this early age when he still had not reached his 27th birthday, Franson already had begun to identify the essentials of a biblical church polity.

Two quotations from his article will illustrate. Drawing a lesson from the potential for serious church conflicts that was present within and between the Corinthian and some of the other New Testament churches, Franson said:

> I believe our ideas will become a lot clearer if we keep in mind that during the days of the apostles the whole executive power lay in the hands of the individual congregations and not in the hands of a denomination, a synod, or a conference.... It is not difficult to see that if we would keep these precedents in mind, the best way to solve the question about the synods would be for each congregation to act as its own synod.

He then pointed out that each local church's acting as its own synod does *not* mean that each local church does not stand in a *responsible* relationship to all the others, although no formal relationship between them had been spelled out. But this raised the question, "Did not the churches then stand in any *formal* relationship to each other?" His answer:

> As far as I have been able to find out, only through the itinerant evangelists, or missionaries. These individuals not

only transmitted the funds that had come in—one from this place, another from that—one for this purpose, another for that—but also these individuals were to stimulate the congregations "to wholesome thinking," and to bring to their minds "the words spoken in the past by the holy prophets and the command given by our Lord and Savior through your apostles" (II Peter 3:1-2); and that command and those words we, of course, have in our Bibles today, and they are complete and not in need of any further clarifying resolutions.

An Unexpected Application in Utah

Fredrik Franson had been planning to go to Sweden the following summer for evangelistic campaigns. But when he came home to Estina to begin his preparations he met a former Mormon who had walked out all the way across the Rockies from Utah. He was deeply stirred by what this man told him, and he thought, "Here there is more need than in any other place." He began to pray that the Lord would send someone out there, but after a few weeks, he realized that he himself must go. He cancelled his trip to Sweden, wrote to his former co-worker in Minnesota, John F. Fredrickson and by October 5, the two of them had begun their work in Salt Lake City.

For nearly ten months these two missionaries labored together in Utah in house-to-house visitation, personal conversations, and in public meetings whenever possible. They were glad to find American-born missionaries there ahead of them, particularly since many of these were also trying to help the Scandinavian settlers. Utah had then nearly twice as many Scandinavians as had Nebraska, but neither the Swedish, Danish, or Norwegian churches, nor any of the revival groups from these countries, had ever sent missionaries out to work among these Utah settlers. When Franson and Fredrickson came to Salt Lake City the local Presbyterian Church asked them as early as their second Sunday there to speak in its evening service in the Scandinavian language.

Utah was difficult. Near the end of their mission Franson

wrote, "We surely have had many dark hours. . . . In several places it has really seemed as if not much fruit appeared after our work. But then in other places we have experienced that God is equally strong in Utah as in other places." This they saw very clearly in Mount Pleasant, a largely Danish town some 90 miles south of Salt Lake City. A young Presbyterian missionary pastor, Duncan McMillan and his wife Judy, had started a day school in this town. They had also started a Sunday school which drew over 200 children. Franson and Fredrickson began their work in Mount Pleasant in November. The Holy Spirit worked with them to bring an awakening, and soon thirty persons had confessed Jesus as Lord and Savior. Persecutions and threats began, but the two missionaries worked with Pastor McMillan teaching the new converts, particularly seeking to develop those who seemed to be gifted for leadership and the spiritual nurturing of the flock. On January 11, 1880 fourteen of these new converts joined in organizing the Mount Pleasant Presbyterian Church electing two of their brethren as elders and two as deacons. That church celebrated its 100th anniversary in January 1980.

The very next day Franson and Fredrickson were at work farther south, in the town of Ephraim. Here again the Lord brought an awakening, and sixteen persons professed faith in Christ. The opposition became fierce. Once a shot was fired into the room where they were meeting. Franson counseled the group of new believers to seek fellowship with Pastor McMillan and the new church in Mount Pleasant. The result was that on February 1, 1880 this group in Ephraim was organized as a local Presbyterian church also.

While in Utah Franson studied Mormonism thoroughly. He became so familiar with its tenets and practices that many Mormons insisted that he himself must be an apostate from Mormonism. He had identified those Scripture verses which the Mormons had misapplied in developing their millennial expectations, particularly those which they taught their missionaries to use. These verses he organized into a Bible study which he urged all Mormons to take, as well as anyone else who had any acquaintance with Mormonism. The following year he published this study in a 212-page Danish book, the title of which translates, "The Craftiness of Deception Exposed: 70 of the Bible Passages Misunderstood by the Mormons, Considered in the Light of the Scripture" (Forförelsens Kunstgreb Afslörede: eller 70 af Mormonernes misforstaaede Bibelsprog betragtede in Skriftens Lys).

A Free Evangelical Church in Denver

Some time in June 1880, Fredrik Franson left Utah for Colorado, a state which then had a booming mining economy. Denver, the capital, had grown from under 5,000 to over 35,000 in ten years. About five hundred Swedes lived there, and the Colorado Swedes were generally known as among the most callous and godless Swedes anywhere. Franson was himself a miner's son from Pershyttan on the iron range above Örebro in Sweden. He had a deep burden for the Swedish prospectors and miners in Colorado. He sought them out in Denver, in Black Hawk, in Georgetown, and even in Leadville and other remote mining communities.

On his first visit to Denver, Franson found the shoemaker Nels Johnson who came through for the Lord. Later he would introduce other new converts to Johnson, and these then began meeting in his home. Soon fifteen were meeting regularly.

On his second visit Franson began to encourage these friends to organize themselves as a local church. They did this on July 26, 1880, using the Moody Church Principles of Organization as a model. The next day they filed their Record of Incorporation with the Clerk of the City and County of Denver. That Record of Incorporation states:

> This body of believers desires to be known only as Christians without any reference to any denomination, yet regarding all who hold and preach the truth contained in our articles of faith as equally belonging to the same Head, and is thereby free to cooperate and unite with them in the carrying out of the work of our common Master.

The church had incorporated in such a way that it could function legally as its own synod, cultivating responsible relationships with other local churches. It is possibly the first Swedish free church incorporation on record anywhere. To Franson this incorporation was a very significant step. He wrote in September:

> A small local church has been in existence here in Denver for some months now with no other designation than that of its locality. It is incorporated under the name: The Scandinavian Church of Denver. They meet "from house to house." Three brothers have been elected and set apart as elders of the church. The church also has given license to a brother, N. F. Pierson, to work among the Scandinavians in Colorado and wherever God may lead him. In doing this, we discovered in a practical way that—whether it be a question of incorporation with the right to hold property, or of a preacher's ordination with the right to perform weddings, etc.—what a single local church does in any of these respects is fully as valid before the law as the acts of any synod or conference. We found this actually to be so in the recording of these transactions.

Franson also was concerned that this church should be kept from divisive, non-biblical doctrines. He wrote in the same report:

> These friends will gladly receive visits from any brother who believes in and serves Jesus. They desire to be one with all who are the brothers and sisters of Jesus, recognizing that they together with them make up one and the same body. They consider that variant concepts about points not vital to the life in Christ ought not to hinder in any way brotherly love or the extension of full brotherly fellowship. Consequently, they have left to each believer individually such questions as, for instance, the different doctrines about the mode, time, and meaning of baptism, so that on these questions each believer may believe and act in accordance with his own best understanding of God's Word, without his therefore having to feel the slightest strangeness from his fellow believers in the flock.

Today this church continues as the Belcaro Evangelical Free Church. It celebrated its 100th anniversary in 1980.

Fruit in Nebraska: Four New Congregations

Not long after his work in Denver, Fredrik Franson was in the center of a powerful revival that moved out from Phelps Centre, Nebraska to communities all around from the end of October through most of November 1880. Phelps Centre and Phelps County had at that time attracted large numbers of new Swedish immigrants and re-settlers. Among these were many Mission Synod and Synod of Ansgar people, Baptists, Methodists, and a large number of Augustana Lutherans. However, only the Mission and Augustana synods had their own church buildings in the area.

On October 1 a group of believers at Phelps Centre had advertised a "free and non-sectarian" mission meeting beginning October 22 and to this Franson had been invited. His Bible studies on the Second Coming of Christ had turned into a "downpour of God's grace." Leander Hallgren, the secretary of the meeting, wrote at the beginning of December, "We have been blessed and blessed and blessed. There have been several meetings from which not one single soul left unsaved." He also reported, "The people here have long limped from one foot to the other . . . but now they are getting strength in their legs. The overwhelming majority have long been thinking about the need for a church founded according to the biblical pattern and now it is happening."

At three different parts of Phelps County and at one place in neighboring Kearney County, Franson began to meet with the new converts to study the pattern of church polity seen practiced in the New Testament. The result was that between November 16 and 25 four new churches were organized: the Church of God at Phelps Centre, the Church of God at Westmark, the Church of God at Industry, and the Church of God in Keene. The first three of these filed their Records of Incorporation in the Office of the County Clerk on December 1, 1880.

How have these churches fared since then? Last year, both the Westmark and the Keene churches celebrated their 100th anniversary. The community of Phelps Centre

soon began to lose its population so a group from the Phelps
Centre church in 1899 organized the Holcomb Evangelical
Free Church, and that church continues strong today. We
never have been able to trace the Industry Church. There is
some recent indication that a remnant of that church may
have been active in the starting of the nearby Loomis Evangelical Free church which was organized in 1886.

Some of Franson's Statements on Biblical Church Polity

What were the particulars of the church polity around
which these four Nebraska churches were organized? An
elaboration of these can be found in the articles by Leander
Hallgren and Fredrik Franson in the December 1880 and
January 1881 issues of *Chicago-Bladet*. A summary may be
found in my *The Doctrine of the Church in the Life and Work
of Fredrik Franson* (Wheaton: TEAM, 1977).[3] These quotations will suffice here:

The purpose of the local church is that all be workers. I
like old Mr. Wesley's slogan, "All at it and always at it!"

If every child of God has been given at least one gift, then
it becomes very important for us not only to know which gift
each member has been given, but also that we fan that gift
into flame.

When a church rigorously seeks to cultivate God's gifts in
each of its members, and then uses every member both in its
general work and in its public ministry in accordance with
these gifts, that which is the church's goal—the strengthening of God's children and the salvation of the lost—is best
achieved.

All may speak to strengthen, encourage, and comfort (I
Cor. 14:3), and all may also be taught and comforted from
such speaking....But the record shows that there were
also certain especially selected persons—those with the
nobler gifts in this one or some other area—who were called
"the elders," and in every congregation these numbered
more than one.

These elders, like all God's children in general, have different gifts—such as those described in Eph. 4:11 and I Cor.
12:28....That these gifts are present in every congrega-

---

[3] This booklet is reproduced in its entirety in Appendix IV.

tion, if only they are drawn out and cultivated, we can readily see even today wherever the Spirit of God is working. We see many at such times who have the gift to shepherd or pastor—often quite unobtrusively—those who are the newly converted....The same is also true with regard to the teaching ministry.

In each local church there are those who have that special gift—the gift of evangelism—the gift to communicate with those still uncoverted....When it is noticed that someone in the church has that gift, then it becomes important that that person be encouraged in every possible way both to deal with souls privately and to witness publicly. And if that person continues to let God's Spirit lead him, he should be encouraged also to go out with an older brother to do some similar witnessing in other places....Many churches have experienced brothers who well could go out like that and witness about Jesus.

God's children in each locality are the preachers who should speak for the mutual strengthening of one another and also to preach to the unsaved there. God seems to have a rule that as long as an evangelist can work with good fruit among the unsaved in a locality, he ought to remain there; and so long as all is well—even if he has to have four or five meetings a day—since God's Spirit is with him. But after that, God's will seems to be that the evangelist "must preach the good news about the kingdom of God in the other towns also"; and when this is done, God's children still seem to fare just as well—even though they are left by themselves to build each other up through those gifts only that exist within the church. Then after some time, perhaps God's Spirit may again have moved in such a way that more people are under conviction; and then God will—in answer to the prayers of his children there—save those people, either without any visiting evangelist, or by sending back the same one who left earlier, or even someone else.

There is one thing I have noticed: when God's children will not make use of the gifts God has given them to His praise, then the devil will get hold of those gifts.

How far from, or how close to, the biblical pattern of church polity—not as I have set it forth here, for in this article I may well have been mistaken; but as we see it depicted in the New Testament—that is a question which each denomination needs to answer for itself....On the other hand, all those who join themselves together in local independent churches must also be careful to show—by their deeds as well as by their fruit—that they are one with all God's children.

Sometimes I have thought that since our Lord's return seems to be so very near, perhaps this is not the appropriate time to speak up on the structuring of the local church. But when we stop to think that both the holding forth of the doctrine of the Lord's return to God's children and working for the salvation of the unconverted are exactly the purposes for which the Church on earth exists, then it becomes very clear that in every locality God's children ought to band themselves together as closely as possible—so that they may utilize with greater zeal the few days left them to serve the Lord efficiently.

Toward the "Any Moment Expectation" of Christ's Return

Fredrik Franson spent the first four months of 1881 in northern Illinois, the cradle of the Swedish-American revival movement. He was to leave soon for Sweden, but first he must arrange for the publication of his Danish book on Mormonism. In the meantime churches all throughout the area of the Mission Synod as well as Synod of Ansgar welcomed him. In Chicago he had series of meetings in both the Southside Tabernacle and the Moody Church.

He found people interested in the theme of Christ's return as well as in the unfulfilled prophecies in general. The Swedish revival people had been said to be traditionally less interested in the doctrine of the last things than were the Germans and the British. However, through his association with the Moody campaigns, Franson had seen how significant this doctrine had been for both the German-American and Anglo-American revival movements. The German theologian Bengel's exegesis of Revelation had provided in the 18th century a refutation of the then reigning Whitbian postmillennialism. It also stimulated significant new energy in the German pietist movement. Bengel's exegesis had been introduced to British and American revival preachers through John Wesley's *Notes On the New Testament*. Both the British and the American revival movements had long been concerned with unfulfilled prophecy and the soon return of Christ.

Franson had mastered the arguments of such *exclusive futurists* as John Nelson Darby and his followers and of the *exclusive historicist* H. Grattan Guinness, both of these within British premillennialism. He also knew the mediating but dramatic positions of Michael Baxter which were somewhere between these two exclusivist positions. Franson also knew American premillennialism. William J. Erdman, Secretary of the Niagara Bible Conference, a pioneer in American premillennialism, was pastor of the Moody Church when Franson joined. Franson also knew the pioneering writings of the German-American Lutheran theologian, Joseph A. Seiss, and his arrival in 1878 at a mediating position between preterist, historicist, and futurist premillennialism. Moreover, Franson had thoroughly studied the reports from the first American premillennial conference in New York in 1878 which included Nathaniel West's informative study, "History of the Pre-millenial Doctrine." Also he had very likely personally met such men as James H. Brookes and William E. Blackstone (W.E.B.). Above all Franson knew the Bible. Directly from the Bible he derived his own conviction of, as well as his case for, the premillennial any moment expectation of Christ's return. Whether this message was thought pertinent to Swedes or not, his own findings were conclusive: whether in Minnesota, Utah, Colorado, Nebraska, or even in Chicago and northern Illinois, that message drew Swedes to repentance, to hope, to encouragement, separation, and mission. And Franson preached it.

Toward the end of February 1881, Franson was asked to take part in a general mission meeting at Moline, Illinois. The announced topics included both church polity and the Second Coming. This was the first meeting on record between Franson and some of the more outspoken proponents of Swedish church reform in northern Illinois. These men held views that were significantly different from those that Franson had advocated and applied in his work on the frontier in the last two years. But the deep spiritual respect among these men did not suffer from this. When the meeting could not finish the questions on the Lord's return, it appointed Franson to work with Professor John Princell and Editor John Martenson in arranging for a special meeting to deal only with that topic.

The committee was able to announce on March 18 that this meeting would be held in Chicago April 13 to 18 and to publish an agenda of sixteen topics. It assigned each topic to one or two persons for the preparation of papers, and these papers were to be the basis for the discussion. Princell and Franson each prepared three papers. Interest in the meeting was great. People came from afar to attend. The discussions proved to be very spirited. No resolutions were adopted, but much useful information was imparted. In all, fourteen of the announced topics were covered.

A few days after the meeting Franson left Chicago for New York enroute finally on his long delayed mission to Sweden. He still was under twenty-nine years of age and, except for these first four months in 1881, he had spent all of the past four years in the remotest parts of the Swedish-American settlement. Yet on May 13 the following notice appeared in *Chicago-Bladet:*

> Would you like to travel to Sweden in good company? We are pleased to announce that Brother F. Franson and some other brothers have secured passage from New York to Sweden on the 21st of this month.

The young Fredrik Franson had now become no less known to and accepted by the Swedes in northern Illinois than to those out on the frontier.

The Founding of the Evangelical Free Church of America

Though nine years were to pass before Fredrik Franson returned to the United States, his labors there continued to bear fruit. In tracing the contributing influences to the rise of the Swedish Evangelical Free Church in America, its 35th anniversary *Minneskrift* states:

> There were other spiritual influences also that had a lasting impact on the Free Friends. Missionary F. Franson's emergence among them was epoch-making. His zeal for the

salvation of sinners, his zealous prayer life, his warm admonitions to search the Bible and particularly to research the prophecies—to which the prophetic conference which he arranged on Chicago's northside in 1881 was a powerful demonstration—all of this from this one God-dedicated man commanded emulation and won for him a host of supporters in the Free Church congregations.

Actually two initiatives had been taken in the fall of 1884 that brought about the final resolution of the church polity tensions that had been building up within the Swedish Lutheran pietist movement in America. One of these was the call issued jointly on November 1, 1884 by the president of the Mission Synod and the pastor of an independent church in Chicago for the formation of a new grouping of churches for organized work. The result was that delegates from various churches of the Mission Synod and Synod of Ansgar and from some independent churches gathered in Chicago, February 18 to 25, 1885, and organized the Swedish Evangelical Mission Covenant of America—today the Evangelical Covenant Church of America. The position of the church was declared to be non-creedal but biblical.

The other initiative was a declaration adopted by the Boone, Iowa meeting, October 14 to 19, 1884. That meeting which was a follow-up of one a year earlier in Chicago had been attended by about twenty delegates from ecclesiastically quite diverse elements within the Swedish-American spiritual awakening such as Lutherans, Baptists, Methodists, Congregational, Holiness, and independents. These delegates had drawn up a declaration of specific biblical teachings concerning the Church on earth. They had issued a call for joint work in missions and social concerns on the basis of this biblical ecclesiology and under God's Word only—and particularly the New Testament—as their "unalterable charter." A follow-up meeting in Minneapolis in March 1885 had further clarified their understanding of mission as well as their adherence to the expectation of Christ's pretribulation, premillennial return.

Around these principles which are quite similar to those which Franson had pioneered on the frontier several years

before, the local churches which are today known as the
Evangelical Free Church of America, began to work together. They called themselves at that time the Fellowship of
Christians for Joint Mission Work ("De kristnas gemensam-
ma verksamhet"). Several of the churches that Franson had
helped to found on the frontier took an active part in this
movement. Dr. Arnold T. Olson, President emeritus of the
Evangelical Free Church of America, writes the following
concerning Franson's part in these developments:

> Fredrik Franson was a pioneer thinker in the struggle for
> an understanding of the New Testament principles of the
> structure of the local congregation and inter-church rela-
> tionships at a time when Scandinavian immigrants from a
> state church environment were struggling with the prin-
> ciples of a congregation in a pluralistic and free society. His
> principles are easily identified in the principles of the
> Evangelical Free Church of America today.

The first missions committee of this movement was set up
at that 1884 meeting in Boone, Iowa. Therefore, the EFCA
Board of Overseas Missions is undoubtedly the oldest foreign mission board in groups significantly influenced by
Franson. Their first overseas missionary was Hans Jensen
von Qualen who arrived in China in 1887.

2

FREDRIK FRANSON AND AGGRESSIVE EVANGELISM IN EUROPE

In Europe Franson entered into a completely new phase of ministry. E. J. Ekman, the Swedish free church pioneer, pointed out: "When Fredrik Franson returned, he came more to harvest than to sow. When he preached it was as if sparks fell from his lips on souls already prepared by God's Spirit." Tens of thousands in Sweden heard him preach, and thousands came through to personal faith in Christ.

But Franson's ministry in other parts of Europe turned out to be as significant as his ministry in Sweden. During the first four years Sweden did actually claim most of Franson's time, but in that period he also had a thirteen-month campaign in Norway and a six-month ministry in Denmark. During the next five years it was Germany that claimed the most of his time, but during these five years he also had ministries in Switzerland, France, Italy, among Armenians in Istanbul, and among Germans settlers in southern Russia and the Baltic states. He always was probing for responsiveness. The reapers must reap when the harvest has ripened.

Franson's ministries in these countries had a two-fold complementary thrust: 1) the premillennial any-moment expectation of Christ's return, and 2) aggressive evangelism. Both were claimed to be "foreign," or "strange," or "Ameri-

can" by Franson's detractors in Europe even though histor-
ically both had had their modern day resurgence, not in
America, but in Europe: premillennialism through the exegesis of the venerable German pietist theologian Johann
Albrecht Bengel (and the English scholars who later built on
his exegesis), and aggressive evangelism through the English
"great awakener" George Whitefield.

The First Eight Months in Sweden

Before Franson landed in Malmö in June 1881, Sweden
had had at least seven decades of a nearly continuous revival movement. During this period faithful evangelism had
been carried out on the model of the sower sowing the seed.
Franson expanded the model to include the reaper gather-
ing the harvest and the fisherman pulling in his nets. Applying the principles he had discovered in New Testament ecclesiology Franson encouraged the whole church to be involved in this ingathering. After his second week in Malmö,
he could write:

> I have been really happy to see how neither the preachers
> nor the believers in this place generally have stood on the
> sidelines as spectators. They have stepped right in and have
> begun to talk with the uncoverted, though clearly for some
> this has been done only after considerable struggle in
> prayer to get over their own inbred resistance to it. But a
> real blessing comes when all God's children can take part in
> this way and help each other not only to throw out the net,
> but, what is just as important—though often neglected by so
> many preachers—to pull in the net once it has been thrown
> out.

After his first five months, he wrote with real joy about
the progress he had seen in this respect. He told about a letter he had received from a brother who had helped in an
after-meeting where seven people had stayed behind and all
seven had been converted. Franson quotes this brother as
follows: "This really got us all sharpened up. Doesn't a
fisherman get excited when he is drawing in his seine and
then sees that there are fish glistening? Doesn't he then
make sure that the fish stay in the seine until he gets them

all ashore?. . . Should we do any less? In our joy in the catch we can't simply leave the fish to die in the net. Shouldn't we also try to get them in. . . to get in as many as possible?"

To Franson, responsible evangelism also required the use of after-meetings—prayer and counseling sessions—immediately after the main message. In this same letter he wrote:

This is the season of the year (winter) when God seems to have his special harvest time. O how important it is at this time that all preachers of the Word "compel" people to Jesus, that after the message they seek to get the anxious ones aside by themselves and, even more than can be done during the message, point out the gracious promises of God to them. The preacher who considers it too embarrassing to do this will not only forfeit many blessed moments down here, but will, I am convinced, also forego many blessed memories in heaven.

For the first eight months Franson worked in the belt across the middle of Sweden from north of Stockholm to the Karlstad area in the west. Hundreds of souls were saved. The press generally gave him good notices. For instance, after his meeting in Linde Mission House on September 3, 1881, *Lindesposten* used more than a full page for a transcription of the message he gave including the invitation. Pastor C. H. Adde of the state church in Vikers also took part in Franson's meetings in this area. Later he wrote: "It has been a joy for me to share in this work in various localities where Fredrik Franson has itinerated and held meetings and to see God's wondrous power manifested. Through his preaching and the grace of God, many souls have been encouraged and given strength to work with greater zeal in the service of the Lord."

The Karlstad Example

However some newspapers began to be critical as people were turning to the Lord in greater and greater numbers. For instance, in Karlstad where people from every level of society flocked to the meetings, and well over 150 people, including some girls who had previously been used in prostitution, were saved in less than two months, stories were printed which later had to be retracted. From the explanatory editorials it became clear that what had really stirred the wrath of the newspaper people was the distinction Franson kept making between "the uncoverted" and "God's children." They were doubly hurt when it became clear to them that the leadership of the missionary association in Karlstad stood firmly with Franson.

The concern of Franson, as well as of the Karlstad Missionary Association at this time, was the need to give true Christian fellowship and nurture to the more than 150 new converts who now were regularly attending the missionary association's meetings in the Bethlehem mission house. When the members of the association realized that this would actually require a complete transformation of the association, they went ahead with it. Here is how that development is reported by Bethlehem's own historian:

> We did not quite know how to receive all these new converts who wanted to join the body of believers—whether in the Mission Association or in the Lord's Supper Association? The question came up for serious discussion at one of our membership meetings. Then Franson went to the pulpit. With all the power of his personal sincerity and spiritual strength he called out, "Dear brothers and sisters, open the door for all believers and newly converted to come in! Should not this mission association constitute itself as a local church according to the biblical pattern?" At that moment throughout the hall an almost unanimous "Yes" was heard. And that question, which otherwise would have taken months, perhaps years, of deliberation, now was resolved in a matter of moments because of the powerful thinking of this clear-sighted man.

At its next annual meeting, January 9, 1881, the association formally ratified that "yes," and that meeting has since been considered the founding date of the Bethlehem Church in Karlstad. The 30th anniversary album of the church states, "In the years that followed, the church kept growing by those who 'got converted when Franson was here.' Certainly there were those who fell away, but even today we still have a number of members who reckon their conversion from that time."

Franson's concern for the guidance and nurture of the newly converted found expression in still another way during this period. It was at Karlstad that he wrote the tract, "Counsel for the Newly Converted," designed to be put into the hands of each newly converted person. This tract has since been translated into many other languages and is still being circulated.

Persecution Unleashed

In February 1881 Fredrik Franson began meetings in another area of Sweden, the many cities and towns to the southwest of Stockholm between Lake Vättern and the east coast. The first city on the itinerary was Norrköping where Leander Hallgren, his friend from Nebraska, joined him. Again the Lord blessed. They had the meetings in two different halls, Franson and Hallgren alternating from night to night. Pastor Lagerqvist from one of the nearby state church parishes also cooperated. Suddenly, however, Franson faced a new situation.

Ekman in his report on Franson's work in Sweden states, "But every day the enmity from a large part of the state church's clergy grew, and at one time it looked very threatening." This enmity was first publicly unleashed in Norrköping. Three state church pastors came to the meeting one night. They stayed for the after-meeting, but, after the initial prayer session and just as the after-meeting itself was getting started, the senior pastor got up, interrupted the meeting, and told the people to go home. According to Ekman, "A rabble which had gathered behind the pastor, by the door, now broke out in a wild fury that must have resembled quite a bit the mob scene at Ephesus." Östgöta-Correspondenten reported, "A terrible tumult resulted. Many tried to speak at once but were hushed down." When the people finally did go home, according to the paper, "an honor guard of one police officer and three constables was already standing there at the door." The pastor later regretted what he had done, but the damage already had been done. After two days the missionary association decided it would be best for Franson to leave town.

Franson moved on to Linköping, the major city in the area. Again the Lord blessed the meetings, but the newspapers began to heap personal abuse on both Franson and local mission association leaders. During the farewell service at the end of the week the dean of the state church and some fellow state church pastors attended. The next morning before Franson left town, he was summoned to a meeting of the state church council. Afterwards he continued through the whole week with his scheduled meetings in the nearby towns, but rumors were circulating that the Linköping state church council had issued an injunction against him. On March 7 the newspapers announced that the Linköping state church council had indeed voted an injunction against Franson, based on an edict of the King from December 1868. On that same day Franson arrived in Skenninge, still farther west.

Östgöten reported in detail on Franson's meeting in Skenninge that night, which was very peaceful except for the disturbances by the local policemen and the city prosecutor who attended the meeting together with the local state church pastor and the state church council. The next day without even calling Franson the state church council voted an injunction against him, also based on the King's edict of December 1868, and the council turned the matter over to the city prosecutor for his implementation. The city prosecutor immediately made Franson's quarters in the courtyard of the mission hall appear, according to *Östgöten's* description, like "a fugitive's hideout under police surveillance." Private prayer meetings were interrupted. The public meeting that night, at which 1,500 people attended, but in which Franson did not preach, was made a disgraceful shambles all in the name of King Oscar II. The next day the city prosecutor summoned Franson to appear in magistrate's court.

The whole tragicomedy ended with the magistrate's court pronouncing Franson not guilty, but it was now evident that segments of the press, the state church clergy, and the civil

authorities were clearly acting together publicly to disrupt
Franson's meetings. With two injunctions on the books
against him Franson realized that he faced a serious new
situation in Sweden. He decided to bypass several towns on
his original schedule and so quickly moved south and then
east to get over as soon as possible to the island of Gotland
where he could pray and plan his next moves. He held a few
meetings along the way, and these, though unannounced,
drew huge crowds. But the press was against him. For instance, when the reporter in the Eksjö meeting heard the
people praying by name for their unsaved family members
and friends, he walked out in disgust and then filed a detailed report with the following comment:

> We consider it the duty of the press to bring this kind of
> unworthy procedure to the attention of the clergy and civil
> authorities.... We have many times in the past advocated
> tolerance between the different congregations that have
> arisen...but when this freedom now entitles individuals in
> an audience to identify themselves as God's children, and to
> publicly pray for their fellow men as if they were hardened
> sinners, then to seek to limit this freedom is in order.

Here then this reporter naively put his finger on exactly
the kind of opposition that Franson was up against, the deliberate effort of the press, the clergy, and the civil
authorities to curtail his and the people's religious freedom.
That was no inconsequential opposition. It was exactly
along this pattern that the opposition did indeed unfold itself
over the next two years, when four more local state church
council injunctions were served on Franson, all based on the
King's edict of December 1868. The last one was served in
the liberal university city of Lund.

Franson's Response

Fredrik Franson's response is instructive. He decided to
appeal the injunctions in court and then, when he had started that process, he immediately went on with his public
evangelism much as before, to which the subsequent injunctions are an eloquent testimony. However, the appeal process became complicated because each court invariably

found in favor of the lower one. Consequently Franson had to appeal to a higher court, and finally to the King. In all but one of the appeals the King found in Franson's favor and struck down the injunctions. In that one exception Franson had been unaware of a certain legal technicality. The verdict in the final case came from the King on August 26, 1884. The legal barriers against aggressive evangelism in Sweden had finally been removed.

Franson responded in another way also. He significantly increased his literature ministry. He filed for and received a license in Uppsala to publish a monthly periodical, *Frälsningens Visshet* (Salvation Assurance). Before the end of March 1882 the introductory issue was out. The magazine did not carry Franson's own articles. Its main features for several months were two series, the one drawing noticeably on the writing of Rosenius, the father of the Swedish revival movement; the other highlighting Origen and the questions he had to answer in the early church.

At the same time Franson authorized publication of the overview he had given of Revelation at Norrköping on February 7, the proceeds to go to the building fund for a new mission hall in that city—in which later the Bethlehem church was founded. He also authorized the third printing of the book of reports from the 1881 Chicago Prophetic Conference. There was no let up in his ministry.

A Visit to England

While Fredrik Franson was doing all this, he also took a trip to England. On May 3, 1882 he was the speaker at the opening breakfast of the annual conference of the National Sunday Schools Union in London. What other purpose there might have been for this trip is not certain, but years later Franson himself told of some very decisive, lasting impressions he personally had received from some of the missionary messages he had heard during these "May Meetings" in London. He also mentioned having been a guest in the home of Mrs. Elizabeth Baxter, co-founder with Pastor Boardman of Bethshan, the home for healing that both Andrew Murray and A. B. Simpson regarded so highly. On May 11, 1882 Fredrik Franson and two Swedish companions were received into membership in the British Branch of the Evangelical Alliance.

Before the end of May, Fredrik Franson was back in Sweden. His public meetings continued unabated till the end of the year. Again there was opposition and he was served with state church injunctions at Halmstad south of Gothenburg, Visby on Gotland island, and Falun in north central Sweden. At Härnösand, to the north along the coast, he spent three weeks of happy service with a former state church pastor who then served as a Swedish Mission Covenant preacher, Fridolf Risberg, a man whose name later was to be indelibly stamped on the first thirty years of TEAM's history.

Shortly after his first arrival in Sweden in 1881, Franson had called for a periodical that would set before the people of Sweden the imminency of Christ's return. That call was now being answered. On December 28, 1882 the introductory issue of the weekly Morgonstjärnan (Star of the Morning) made its appearance, published by Franson's friend, August Hedström of Örebro. This first issue contained an article by Franson entitled "An Appeal for Workers." Franson became a frequent contributor to this paper. Many of his Bible studies appeared in it serially.

The Norway Campaign

On January 1, 1883 Fredrik Franson began his ministry in Norway. He went there in response to an invitation from the Free Christian Congregation and Missionary Association in Oslo. The invitation had been conveyed to him through the lay preacher C. B. Falck, Field Secretary of the Joint Association of the Free Mission Movement, who also was a member of this church.

After a month in Oslo, Franson embarked on a ministry to several cities southwest of Oslo, then down along the coast, and, for a full seven months, all the way around the coast and north as far as Hammerfest. The return schedule took five months.

Everywhere crowds came to the meetings, and in each city anywhere from a score to over a hundred persons were converted. The securing of halls was a problem at times. Some halls were withdrawn because of the after-meetings. In some places Lutheran lay preachers or state church pastors stood behind such actions. The press reported the meetings variously. The national circulation right wing daily *Aftenposten* reported on one meeting in Oslo which, it estimated, was attended by some 1,700 people. "But," the report stated, "of these, at least 1,400 apparently belonged to the lowest classes." The whole report was slanted and condescending, but toward the end the reporter said, "I have written down the above, because these meetings in Oslo's labor hall are surely to be a part of our cultural and church history."

Carl F. Wisløff gave this evaluative report in *Norsk Kirkehistorie* (Oslo: 1971) III, p. 52:

> Franson at once began to use methods that had proved effective elsewhere. All of God's children were asked to rise. Then there would be a prayer meeting. This would be followed by the "after-meeting."
> This new meeting technique caused a sensation. On the part of some it was criticized. Then, as well as later, many have had little faith in such methods. . . . Nevertheless, it must be said that after-meetings—although in some subdued form—have been taken into use in all camps both within the state church and among the free churches.
> Franson and the course he took led to a change in the thinking about the church and the confessional awareness of many confessing Christians.

The Background

In a few places in Norway, the local Lutheran free church or the local Lutheran prayer house committee sponsored Franson's meetings. However, in most places it was the local free mission group or congregation that assumed the sponsorship. These were either dissenter congregations or the offshoot of dissenter congregations founded in the 1850's through the revivals associated with Pastor Gustav

Adolf Lammers in Skien.

Pastor Lammers had early recommended to those churches the principles of the then existing evangelical free
churches in Switzerland, France, and Germany, particularly the principle of freedom of conscience for the individual
believer as to the time and mode of baptism. In 1863 these
"Lammers Churches" had actually adopted that principle,
but they had also continued to maintain a public image as
dissenter churches, not merely fulfilling the special
registration legally required of them as dissenter congregations. After twenty or more years these churches now saw
clearly that this policy was hindering both their evangelistic
effectiveness in the society and any signficant church
growth on their part. Therefore at their Joint Association
meeting in July 1882 they had taken an action which they
hoped would make possible a reversal of this downward
trend, and it was from this new position they had decided to
call Fredrik Franson to Norway.

What had happened was that on January 1, 1882 the Lammers congregation in Oslo and the Swedish Ansgar Society
in Oslo had merged, calling themselves the Christian Free
Congregation and Missionary Association. The merger
agreement had included the principle of freedom of conscience for each individual member as to his future relationship to the state church, a principle long honored in the
Swedish revival movement. From now on formal personal
dissent or non-dissent from the state church was not to be
an issue in acceptance for membership. The congregation
would function both as a formal church membership for
legal dissenters who had resigned from the church and as a
missionary association that would include both dissenters
and non-dissenters. When this local merger agreement was
ratified by the July 1882 Joint Association meeting it was
understood that this principle would become policy throughout the Free Mission Movement in Norway.

With this principle accepted, the churches immediately
saw a door opened to them for combining effective local
evangelism with the needed biblical nurture and guidance

of the newly converted. They would set up missionary societies alongside the church organizations, in which the newly converted could join and take part and there find the needed Christian fellowship and nurture, without having to formally resign from the state church and become dissenters. The old Lammers churches saw a new day ahead of them.

One member of the Oslo church at that time was Miss Cathrine Juell, a member of a prominent Oslo family, who, during her travels in the United States in the 1870's, had attended some of the D. L. Moody meetings and had become "radically converted." She got to know Franson at that time, and now in the new situation facing the old Lammers churches she recommended him as just the man to minister among them.

Franson had no problem with this new policy that these churches had adopted. His procedure was simple. Toward the end of each meeting series he would ask the older and newer believers if they did not think it would be necessary for them to work together in one missionary association if they were to further God's cause in their community in the best way? If the answer was "Yes," he would say, "Well then, let's get it done right away." And in almost every place he was able to help them get a missionary association organized. The new converts would then join this group, in some places 30 to 80 and in others as many as 150 or 200 or even 250. In some associations they were able to begin immediately with Sunday schools or singing groups or district prayer meetings and women's groups.

Franson saw a particular need for literary links among the many new groups of believers in Norway. He immediately commissioned work on the compilation of a Norwegian gospel songbook that would include translations of both American and Swedish favorites. This new songbook, *Evangelii Basun*, was ready for use by the fall of 1883. Franson also suggested to C. B. Falck that he undertake the publication of a periodical for the Free Mission Movement. Falck accepted this, and on April 15, 1883 the introductory issue of the semi-monthly *Morgenrøden* (Morning Glow) was sent out. This periodical, too, became a frequent and important channel for Franson's Bible studies and messages.

Franson's Parting Counsel and the Founding of the Mission Covenant of Norway

When Fredrik Franson left Norway after thirteen months, he wrote a farewell message—a pastoral letter—to the many groups of newer and older believers he left behind in the country. In this letter he discussed particularly the principles and functions of the missionary associations. The letter was published in *Morgenrøden* in six installments between February and April 1884. Following are a few excerpts:

While these missionary associations thus reach out their hands to all God's children, and in that respect are as universal as possible, they do, on the other hand, screen very particularly so that no one who does not have the life in Christ should join. Their desire is that these associations be composed of persons who are spiritually alive, and not be a mixture of some dead and some alive. In this respect, these associations desire to be as narrow as possible. Their motto is that *none* who do not belong to Christ, but *all* who do belong to Him, may join.

Without attaching themselves to any particular name, these associations desire to exercise just as strict a discipline over their members as do any of the other organized congregations. They desire and pray that their preachers, district leaders, Bible women, as well as each individual member, may be filled with the Holy Spirit; and they wish—and they also have been given to see—sinners both saved and preserved.

But we see here the necessity for these associations to have specific meetings where the believers may have opportunity to get to know each other, and where the whole congregation may become aware of the life and walk of each individual member. Such meetings could also be of particular help to any who may have fallen, or perhaps give the opportunity for any correction or restoration that may be needed. But in order to maintain this type of effective discipline, it is necessary to keep up a correct membership list (possibly with membership cards in larger cities).

Each missionary association ought to support two workers, one to serve in its own immediate community, and the other to itinerate and develop groups in the surrounding communities.

In order to have a more steady and orderly ministry, it will be necessary also for all the missionary associations in the country to join together in a mission society.

It has hurt me to find out that in some places the inquirers' counseling meetings after the preaching have been discontinued. . . . In the parable of the lost sheep, on account of which the shepherd left the ninety-nine, one lesson Jesus seems to be teaching us is that if ninety-nine believers and one unbeliever were to be together in one meeting, then the most important attention needs to be given to the one.

To you brothers and sisters who have means, let me say once more: use your means as much as possible in the service of God and our Lord Jesus Christ. Send out Bible women and preachers. . . . Think about Norway's interior! May the Word of Truth soon penetrate the darkness that rests over its rural population.

Before the final installment of Franson's letter appeared, the Board of the Joint Association had already drawn up its recommendations. On April 1, 1884 it published a call for a meeting of delegates in the first half of July to consider the Association's future goals and tasks. It also submitted a draft proposal for a constitution. The result was that on July 8, 1884 the Joint Association of the Free Mission Movement reorganized itself as the Mission Covenant of Norway ("Det Norske Misjonsforbund").

New Thinking on the Saving of the Harvest
From Norway Franson went directly to southern Sweden where he ministered the next four months. Besides being served with his sixth injunction in Sweden—from the state church council in the university city of Lund (the council did include a learned doctor!)—he also had to help alleviate some tensions that had developed in Malmö because of the work of a young lady evangelist, Miss Nelly Hall. He wrote, "This gave me also a certain restraint of spirit." He became very concerned, however, when he realized that the prob-

lem was due not so much as to whether a lady had the right to do evangelistic work, but because Christians who had differing views on the question became so intolerant of one another.

In Kristianstad he also discovered another sister engaged in evangelistic work. He began to look at the question in a larger framework, in terms of the size of the harvest, and that in Scandinavia as well as all over the world the time to harvest is now. He then wrote:

> Brothers, the harvest is great and the laborers are few. If the ladies want to help out in the fields during the harvest time, then I think we should let them bind as many sheaves as they can. It is better that women bind the sheaves, than that the sheaves get lost. When one has been sent out on the field and heard the real cries for help from dozens of places, places to which one cannot possibly reach, then one cannot help but think, "It seems strange that only such a few verses of Scripture, about which there are so many disputes, should be made such obstacles to hinder those who otherwise would have responded to these calls for help." But God will direct in this matter also according to His will.

Fredrik Franson was 100% the aggressive evangelist, but he was not a blindly aggressive evangelist. He was a thinker, analyst, problem solver, and strategist. These factors had characterized his aggressive evangelism on the American frontier, in Norway, and certainly also in Sweden; and now they were once more coming into significant play. He asked not merely, "What went wrong with the harvest?" but, "How can the harvest still be saved?" Emigration from Sweden to America had at that time been at its peak for some years. Franson thought about this also, and on May 10, 1884 he wrote from Jönköping:

> Sometimes almost a whole local congregation has left for America, and I have wondered if God wouldn't perhaps at times put it into the heart of a congregation to leave instead for Africa, India, China, Japan, or—if they don't want to go quite that far—to Persia, Russia, or Spain. . . . When so many can go to Africa, China, and the many such places to make money, then others can go there also—to settle and be missionaries in the process.

And what about the harvesting in Sweden, Norway, Denmark, and Finland? One thing that had gone wrong was that many young people who did have a call from God to go out into His service were deliberately discouraged from doing so by older Christians. They were told that they suffered from "preaching sickness," and now many of them could be found in their home communities serving with only minimal blessing. What could be done now? Franson finally opened his heart to reveal a new thrust, a thrust that henceforth was to become a characteristic component of all his ministry. He wrote:

> While on the one hand I have seen the great need for many preachers to go out, on the other hand, I have found during my travels that in almost every community there are some who were strongly led to go. They have felt in need of some further guidance, or they may not have been able to afford or had the time or opportunity to take a full course at some missionary training school. Seeing this, I have long had it on my mind that a three to four week evangelist course could be of great blessing to such people. The great need for witnesses, particularly in Norway and Denmark, has led me to the conclusion that I should try in Jesus' name to make an attempt in this direction during the coming summer.

The First Evangelist Course

The course was to be designed for young men. It was to be non-sectarian. Franson wrote: "None need fear that he will be influenced to adopt any other conviction than he has in any respect, except in such matters as are an integral part of the course, namely, instantaneous conversions, post-message counseling sessions, love for all believers, hastening the Lord's return, and so on." He made plans to hold four trial courses to begin with—at Oslo, Norway, and Västerås, Jönköping, and Malmö, Sweden.

The dates were not announced until the beginning of July. The Oslo course was to begin July 10 immediately after the founding sessions of the Norwegian Mission Covenant. The last course, at Malmö, would begin October 2. Franson also announced at this time that "since my own reservations in this matter have been lifted," sisters also will be welcome.

Despite the short notice forty persons attended the Oslo course, eleven of them ladies. Some of those who attended later became well known leaders in the free evangelical movement in Norway. Of particular note was the riding master Hans Guldberg who in 1887 became one of the three co-founders of the Oslo-based Norwegian Mission in China, the country's first mission society for China, today the Norwegian Evangelical Orient Mission. Another was Cathrine Juell, who later served for fifteen years as a Bible woman in Denmark. A third was Sophie Reuter who sought out Fredrik Franson during his meetings in Kristiansand, in southern Norway, and who shortly after the course left for England with her friend Anna Jakobsen to become missionaries to China with the China Inland Mission. They became Norway's first missionaries to China as well as China Inland Mission's first missionaries from the Continent.

The Denmark Campaign

The Malmö course was hardly over when, on October 17, 1884, Franson appeared in Copenhagen ready to begin his campaign in Denmark. He had made some preliminary contacts while attending the international conference of the Evangelical Alliance in Copenhagen, August 30 to September 7—between the Västerås and Jönköping evangelist courses—and these contacts he had followed up through correspondence. However, after a week in Copenhagen it was clear that he had completely misread the situation. He would have to make a new start under different sponsorship. This turned out to be the year-old Christian Tract Association founded by N. P. Lang, an acquaintance from the February 1881 meeting in Moline, Illinois. Lang, however, had returned again to the United States shortly after founding the association. Despite these extraordinary setbacks, Franson still continued to pray and trust the Lord for a "national moving" in Denmark. Through personal evangelism in this waiting period he had won a core group of friends "one by one," and this group grew to include some older Christians as well.

After Franson had secured a firm rental contract on the fairly large Moravian Meeting House for four nights a week all through November, December, and January, he opened his campaign with preliminary meetings in four different districts of Copenhagen during the last six days of October. When the campaign proper got started he continued with six meetings a week in these four different districts in addition to the four weekly meetings in the Moravian Meeting House. His co-workers included August Nielsen from Bergen, Norway, the Bible woman Cathrine Juell from Oslo, and, after Christmas, F. Johansson from Stockholm. Others also are mentioned, including a Mrs. Nielsen who later served in Africa as a missionary.

How did the Danes respond to Franson's meetings? A Methodist pastor who went to the meetings with his unsaved brother (who did then get saved) wrote:

> Franson was a soul on fire, and his preaching was a reflection of this. A great awakening soon developed. People from all around gathered in such great numbers that the Meeting House, which probably could take about a thousand, was filled to capacity evening after evening. Every night they had after-meetings, and many were won for the Lord.

A farmer who attended five of the meetings wrote: "Franson's skill in leading people to Christ was especially great. . . . Many people developed strong Christian traits that remained with them for the rest of their lives. . . . The crowds streaming to the meetings were huge."

Many sick also came to be prayed for, and God healed some. One day the 70-year old Count Frederik Vilhelm Dannemand, son of the late King Fredrik VI, came with his countess. Soon so many sick were coming that they had to be prayed for in groups. Franson was amazed at the evident display of God's power.

During these meetings Franson also published a Danish edition of the songbook, *Evangelii-Basun,* now expanded to 360 songs. Cathrine Juell helped with the financing of this project.

The meetings in the Moravian Meeting House came to an

end on January 29, 1885. The next day, meeting in the hall of the Christian Tract Association, this association reorganized itself as the Copenhagen Christian Missionary Association ("Kjøbenhavns Christelige Missionsforening"). The membership stood at about 200. F. Johansson was called as the association's pastor.

Opposition Takes a Serious Turn

Franson then planned a week of meetings in Helsingør, north of Copenhagen, and two weeks in the Mørkøv region, about twice as far west from Copenhagen as Roskilde. He also planned to begin meetings in Aarhus on the Jylland peninsula on February 24. After the week in Helsingør, he left August Nielsen to carry on the work there. In the Mørkøv region the national director of the Church Society for Inner Mission in Denmark had given orders that use of the society's prayer houses be denied Franson's meetings. Most of the meetings were held, therefore, in the surrounding farming hamlets, a different one each night and sometimes two in a day. On Sunday and Monday, February 15 and 16, the meetings were held at Count Dannemand's Aastrup Estate near Roskilde. That Sunday nearly a thousand people gathered and many sick came to be prayed for and anointed.

On Tuesday Count Dannemand learned that, on account of an alleged injury to a person prayed for on Sunday at his estate, the local state church pastor had met on Monday night with members of the church council and a medical doctor on the nearby estate of Count Dannemand's niece where the count's sister also was living, and while still on that estate, the doctor had drawn up his medical report. Later that same night the state church pastor had drawn up a formal charge to be filed against Franson. Count Dannemand immediately understood the seriousness of these events and he and his countess wrote out the following statement:

We, the undersigned, hereby testify that we urged Mr. Franson to come to Aastrup because so many in this district wished, both on account of frailties and religion, that Mr. Franson should come, so that they might receive healing and hear his message.

Aastrup, February 17, 1885   (signed) F. V. Dannemand
                                               W. Dannemand

For four days nothing happened. Franson continued his scheduled meetings, and these were favorably reported in the press. However, on Saturday, February 21, Franson was served with a notice to appear in court in Roskilde on Monday. So began a strange court proceeding in which the judge was interested only in the prosecution testimony—when this was not damaging to the prosecution case. The petition of the local people in support of Fredrik Franson as well as the testimonies of well known persons from other parts of Denmark were not considered. Moreover, the judge refused to accept Fredrik Franson's bond money of 500 kroner and instead ordered him held in jail.

For thirty-eight days Fredrik Franson remained in jail. Hearings were held, but during the entire proceedings not one single defense witness was heard. Other irrelevant material, however, was entered into the case.

According to Emil Larsen who researched the above data, Justice Minister Nellemann was contacted. He finally informed the judge that, after correspondence with the Foreign Department, the Justice Department had decided that Franson be banished from the land without suit, "with the provision that he not appear in the land again." After this, the final court hearing was held on Saturday, April 4, 1885, when the judge informed Franson of the justice minister's decision. The judge gave him until April 11 to leave the country, "with the provision that he hold no public meeting in the land during this time." Research shows that Franson never again involved himself in public meetings for healing, though he personally believed that he should continue to pray for the sick.

Franson left immediately for Copenhagen where he and his friends planned for the future of the work and initiated some appeals for the rescinding of the banishment order.

Emil Larsen's account has this final wrap-up:

Neither the conversations with the Justice Minister Nelle-mann, nor the two approaches to the King gave positive results. On Saturday, April 11, Fredrik Franson must take leave of his friends and co-workers in Denmark. But his work for the revival movement in our country did not end thereby. His first action on landing in Sweden is to make provision for the continuation of the work.

The Founding of the Mission Covenant of Denmark

Fredrik Franson, early in his Denmark campaign, had begun to appeal for funds for the building of a mission hall in Copenhagen, and in February *Morgonstjernan* could announce that some 5,000-6,000 kroner had come in for this purpose. Now Franson expanded this appeal to included the sending and supporting of preachers also. He wrote: "The friends who want to help avenge me on Denmark can do so best by helping to support preachers there." For this purpose he set up local committees in both Malmö and Stockholm. The Stockholm committee was able by June 1885 to send the young evangelist G. W. Gillén to Denmark where he worked effectively for two years. Franson's own co-workers also stayed on: August Nielsen for three years, and Cathrine Juell and F. Johansson each for fifteen years.

The work continued to register steady growth. In 1886 J. Jensen-Maar, a local leader from Thisted, was set apart as the first Danish evangelist in the movement. On June 3, 1888 delegates from several of the local congregations met at Aalborg and organized the Mission Covenant of Denmark ("Det danske missionsforbund"). By the following January the organization was able to begin publishing its own periodical, *Morgen-Stjernen* (The Morning Star).

A Wider Responsiveness in Sweden

When Fredrik Franson resumed his evangelistic work in Sweden he discovered that there was far wider responsiveness than before. After having had meetings in Malmö, Landskrona, Linköping, and Norrköping, he arrived in

Stockholm where most of his meetings were held in the 2,000 seat New Church auditorium. He wrote:

> What a difference between Stockholm and Copenhagen! It seems as if the true religion of Jesus has caught hold among both the higher and lower levels of society, and the Gospel is being preached...in a great many meeting places. Nevertheless, regardless of how much one works and preaches, and during this session of Riksdag many believing representatives have also been preaching in different mission halls, it seems as if it is hard to meet the ever growing cravings of the people to hear the Word of God. One must adjust oneself to preach three to four times on Sunday. On coming Ascension Day, I expect to have to speak at five or six meetings.

On May 18, 1885, Franson began an evangelist course in Stockholm. He advertised it as being similar to the previous four, but the announcement indicates that this time the studies are to be particularly concentrated on how to win "the unsaved masses" for Christ. He must have been one of the first evangelists in all Scandinavia to publicly aim for such a goal! The daily course schedule was from 6:00-8:30 a.m. and 5:00-6:30 p.m. followed by preaching service at 7:30 p.m. The Stockholm paper *Hemlandsvännen's* reporter visited the classes several times and published this report:

> We have been well impressed with Franson's deep piety and humility. He is surely not the one-sided, fanatical man which many, who do not know him, but who have been influenced by newspapers and rumors and by the opposition and persecutions unleashed against him in many places, have thereby in advance been led to believe.

Fredrik Franson was now thirty-three years old. Four and a half years earlier in the article on ecclesiology from the revivals in Phelps and Kearney countries, Nebraska, he had written that it is the responsibility of the local believers in any one locality to minister God's Word for each other's mutual upbuilding, and also to preach the Gospel to the unconverted in their area. (See page 27.) A few years later, he would be reminding candidates and new missionaries that God's blessing upon their work in their own "Jerusalem" is not a sign that they are to stay on there, but rather that now they are ready to move on to "Judea," and so on "through the stations," till they come to "Samaria," and finally, to "the uttermost part of the earth."

Fredrik Franson's First Germany Campaign

Fredrik Franson was now clearly applying this principle of outreach to himself. Shortly after having begun his ministry in Stockholm he wrote to C. B. Falck in Oslo that he was hoping to come to Norway in the fall. However, the next primary information found on Franson is his August 18 letter from Barmen, Germany where he had just attended the "Wuppertaler Festwoche" (Wuppertal Evangelical Festival Week). He must by then have been in Germany about two months, for he mentioned having gone through six weeks of German language studies during which time he audited the lectures of Professors Christlieb and Lemme at Bonn University and had also done some other visiting. In other words, he must have left for Germany almost immediately after the evangelist course in Stockholm.

In a later letter Franson mentions having studied German during his 38-day imprisonment in Denmark, so moving on to Germany was not a new or sudden idea. It may be that the Lord had for some time been speaking to him specifically about a ministry in other countries of Europe. Even his joining the Evangelical Alliance in London in 1882 and the contacts he made with European evangelical leaders during the international meeting of the Alliance in Copenhagen in 1884 need perhaps all be seen as parts of a deliberate preparation process. Anyway, we now suddenly find Franson in Germany already well launched in a new phase of his evangelistic ministry.

Franson had brought with him a letter of introduction to Pastor F. W. Krummacher from a believing pastor in Stockholm. He had also stayed in Pastor Krummacher's home during the 1885 Wuppertaler Festwoche. Franson was particularly happy about having attended this festival week because during this week organizations from all three of the German protestant national church denominations, Lutheran, Reformed, and United, had met together. Franson himself had been asked to address four different gatherings during the week.

After this Wuppertal Week Franson visited briefly at the Neukirchen Children's and Missionary Home northwest of Düsseldorf, where a good relationship soon developed between him and Director Mandel. He then moved out to a family in the country for a few weeks of more concentrated German language and Bible studies. Then Director Mandel introduced Franson to Karl Polnick, a young and joyful Christian merchant in Barmen, who with a group of fellow believers operated a Christian reading room on one of Barmen's busiest streets. In the middle of September 1885, Franson began a three months' evangelistic campaign throughout the Ruhr area by arrangement of Pastor Fritz Coerper, Director of the Elberfeld based Evangelical Society for Germany. Series of meetings were held in Solingen, Essen (twice), Mühlheim, Elberfeld-Barmen (5 weeks), Witten, and elsewhere.

After-meetings also were held, but "under the greatest care" and almost always in a side room. But newspapers began to inveigh against these meetings, particularly the children's meetings, and soon some pastors followed suit. But other pastors, and particularly Pastor Fritz Coerper, kept supporting Franson. On November 3, 1885, Franson wrote of Pastor Coerper, "God bless that man! He has stood forth like a man in Christ in defense of these meetings."

Franson was full of praise to God for the souls saved. He generally didn't report on the numbers, but a later letter revealed that in Elberfeld "about a hundred seemed to have found peace with God." In Barmen there also was a great awakening. Did the results last? That, of course, only the Lord knows. However, in 1917 the Chrischona missionary August Kmitta wrote as follows about this awakening:

> A large movement developed at this time in the area around Barmen. Whole crowds of people surrendered to the Lord in Franson's meetings. That not all would stay true was clear from the first. However, it has been very unjust to call it all a "straw fire." . . . Thirty years have now passed since

those events. Not long ago in that area, an audience with some 4-500 people present was asked who among them had come to faith at this time through Brother Franson, and some twenty persons stood to their feet.

But for Franson the pillar of cloud was moving and leading towards southern Germany. By the middle of December he was in Karlsruhe and Durlach where many, both young and old, found the Lord. Over Christmas and through New Year's Eve he was in Strasbourg, Alsace. On New Year's Day 1886 he left for Stuttgart where during the week of prayer he was together with a group of "liberated souls" in an old Reformed church. There too a large number of souls surrendered to Christ. He then went up to Heilbronn where during three evenings "a harvest" was brought in. Before he returned to Stuttgart he also had meetings in Ludwigshafen, Pforzheim and several places in that area including Stammheim and Heimsheim. Three meetings were scheduled for him in the Friedenskirche (Peace Church) in Esslingen over the weekend of January 23 and 24, 1886.

The *Esslinger Zeitung* makes these comments on Franson's activities in the Stuttgart area at this time:

> The appearance of a Swedish missionary and evangelist (Franson), a student of the well known Moody, may well have been among the contributing factors to the religious uplift and revitalization during this season. This may also have been due to his practical presentation and application of the Word. Anyway this much is certain, he was used to call forth a deep religious movement among those present, an inquiring and searching for the highest things, in which so many today, because of the pressures and stresses of their everyday lives, have lost interest.

> Nor did he leave out the school youth. He held special meetings for them, emphasizing particularly the need for obedience to parents. Also in this area a special blessing was detected, and we dare say that this will certainly make easier the burden of church and school, as well as of the home, in the training of these young people.

In Switzerland

From March through August 1886, Franson used the Spittler Book Store in Basel, Switzerland as his address. In the spring he had some meetings in the Basel area. At that time Franson met Director Rappard of the Pilgrim Mission at St. Chrischona, who asked Franson to come to the annual Chrischona conference in July to share his testimony. Franson did this, and he also shared his testimony at the Methodist conference shortly afterwards. Earlier in the summer he had attended the Basel Mission conference. Basically, his stay in Switzerland was for personal rest and spiritual and emotional refreshment. He also undertook to learn French for an evangelistic probe into France.

The France and Italy Campaigns

As early as September Franson began to conduct meetings in French in the western and southern parts of Switzerland. Then in November he moved over to Lyon and St. Etienne in France and so began a five months' ministry which took him in a huge arc, first south to the areas around Nimes where he ministered all through December 1886, over to Marseilles, then back westward to the department of Tarn, on to Toulouse, and through Pau to Orthez, then northward to Bordeaux, and still farther north as far as Moncoutant. He worked with the McAll Mission, the Wesleyans, Baptists, and Salvation Army, as well as with the French Evangelical Free churches that were found in many of these areas. He also worked with individual spiritually concerned pastors of French Reformed churches.

Souls were won for Christ in most places, in some meetings as many as eight or ten. In every place Franson tried to conduct at least one children's meeting, and he was happy about the response from young people and children. He also introduced after-meetings, and despite some criticism and resistance, these were generally accepted, as subsequent reports and editorials in several of the magazines of these groups show. *Evangelical Christendom* in England carried this report from Pastor Louis-D. Martin in Vabre, Tarn:

> The passage of Mr. Franson, the Swedish evangelist, in the mountainous parts of the Tarn has been a blessing to many. The work done by his means is truly that of the Holy

Ghost. He has brought to the knowledge of the Lord many souls now walking in the paths of righteousness and life. Dead formalists and inebriates have been raised from their lethargy, delivered, and freed from slavery of sin. Among our catechumens, seventeen have given themselves to the Lord and rejoice us by their seriousness, their spirit of prayer, and by the patience with which they bear the scorn and nicknames showered on them by their former friends.

At the beginning of April 1887 Franson together with Pastor Élie Vernier of Valence, south of Lyon, set out on a joint mission to visit the old Waldensian churches in the Alpine valleys of northwestern Italy. From a summary which *Evangelical Christendom* made of Vernier's report, comes the following quotation:

> During twenty-five days, the evangelists held fifty meetings in five parishes of the Valleys. Everywhere the presence of God was felt; sometimes all were in tears. A considerable number took the decisive step, and have begun to live for God. Prayer meetings were instituted to give opportunity of grouping together around the Lord the new converts with old Christians now revived, to receive fresh strength day by day, to work, each in his sphere, for the conversion of others.

Among Armenians, Germans, and Jews in Southeastern Europe

After the Italy ministry Vernier and Franson parted, and Franson took a tour of historic sites in Italy, Egypt, Palestine, and Asia Minor, arriving in Istanbul on June 10, 1887. He found a large group of Armenians there that were responsive to the Gospel. He became very conscious again of the need for workers. The Armenians asked him to stay on and minister among them. He also received an invitation to come up into Bulgaria. He himself was deeply burdened by the potential he saw in developing evangelistic ministries among the perhaps several million German settlers inside Russia. From where would the workers come? He wrote:

> There are one and a half billion people in the world today. Let us suppose that each missionary can assume responsibility for telling the Gospel to, and nurture the new converts among 1,500 people. We would need an army then of one

million missionaries. However, whether we have more or perhaps not as many as one million Spirit filled believers in the world today, that is the question.

Franson soon went on to Odessa in southern Russia, spent about a month ministering in the German settlements out on the surrounding steppes, and then left for East Prussia, stopping along the way at Kischeneff to meet Josef Rabinowitz, the leader of the Bessarabian Jewish Christian movement. He arrived at Königsberg (today Kaliningrad) July 21.

The Campaign in East Prussia and Surrounding Areas

Fredrik Franson began a campaign in the eastern German area which lasted for six months. However, his first attention was to Lithuania working out from Memel (now Klaipeda). In the fall he concentrated on East Prussia. As always, he was the aggressive evangelist. God blessed his after-meetings, and many souls were saved.

In October 1887 the missionaries of the Pilgrim Mission (St. Chrischona) asked Franson to be the evangelistic speaker for their week of special services dedicating their first mission hall in Elbing (now Eblag) not far from Gdansk. A report in *Gemeinschaftsbote* stated that each night two different men spoke between 8 and 9 o'clock, and then Franson spoke from 9 to 10 o'clock. The report continued as follows:

First he gave a forceful sermon, in which he mentioned pressing reasons for not putting off one's conversion. He told conversion stories and spoke convincingly of the all-embracing love of Jesus, the great Savior of sinners. The effect of such words was felt throughout the whole hall. Heads were bowed, and many tears ran. . . . Afterwards the opportunity was given for the people in the congregation to pray; and now from all sides of the hall you could hear the believers audibly praying for their unconverted brothers, sisters, parents, children, relatives, and acquaintances. Then those who desired to turn to the Lord and seek peace through his atoning blood were asked to come and sit in the front rows. At the same time God's children, that is the older Christians, were urged to pray. Now a lot of praying was done; many heard for the first time in their lives these words come audibly from their own lips: "Lord be merciful to me a sinner! Have mercy on me!"...

Missionary Franson has in the course of this week become very dear to us. The brethren acknowledged that they had learned a lot from him.... Some of the older Christians have made some comments against the way he proceeds. This has made me think of the seaman who saved a drowning person, but then his friends criticized him for not having grabbed the drowning man according to the right rules that should apply in that particular situation, which they apparently had learned. But the person who was saved just stood there rejoicing, thankful that someone had come to his rescue. The harvest is great, but the laborers are few.

Chrischona missionary August Motzkus, in charge of the work at Elbing, gave the following information: "On the recommendation of Brother Polnick in Barmen, Brother Franson came to East Prussia for the first time in the fall of 1887 to district treasurer Kleinfeldt in Zinten. From there he came to Elbing where he held evangelistic services in our mission hall, October 9 to 14. His method was new and somewhat strange to us; nevertheless, God blessed his work. My diary contains the following entry: 'The Lord has gloriously acknowledged the work of his servant (Brother Franson). Many souls have found God these days with prayer and supplication. The congregation received a refreshing visitation and was greatly blessed. There was no opposition among us here, as there has been in a number of other places in Germany.' Fredrik Franson came back a second time that same year, holding evangelistic meetings in Elbing and its surrounding area, this time also with good results."

Franson was becoming more and more concerned at this time because so many older Christians in Germany did not seem to understand or wish to accept the use of after-meetings in connection with the evangelistic services. However, he remembered that two years earlier in the Elberfeld area, after he had given a message on the biblical basis of after-meetings, Pastor Fritz Coerper had become a strong supporter and had personally attended the meetings whenever possible. He realized the need once more to get this biblical teaching before the Lord's people. Therefore,

while at Zinten, he prepared and published a 48-page booklet, *Die Nachversammlungen, betrachtet im Lichte der Bibel*
(After-meetings Considered in the Light of the Bible). This
booklet is not only a defense of after-meetings, it is an ex-
cellent general presentation of the biblical principles of
evangelism. It was published in Swedish the following
spring in an 84-page "free translation" by Nelly Hall.

After East Prussia, Franson went to Berlin at the invitation of Counts Andreas von Bernstorff and Eduard von
Pückler. He held meetings in their halls and also in a national church chapel. While in Berlin Franson received an
urgent call to come to Norway to conduct more evangelist
courses in order to train needed new workers there.

A New Rural Missionary Outreach in Norway

Fredrik Franson returned to Oslo on February 12, 1888,
four years after his last previous visit. The capital was alive
with evangelistic activities. A report in *Morgenrøden* states:

> All of the local Christian organizations are engaged in
> lively activities, and sinners are awakened and saved almost
> everywhere. . . . And the Salvation Army has come in. . .
> which despite all of its human trappings has, nevertheless,
> been the means of conversion for thousands. . . . And then
> we have Franson, who five years ago was the first among us
> to use the so-called Moody methods. . . . He set the power
> and life of Christianity before the sinner, who had to bend
> his knee and pray God for grace and the forgiveness of sins.
> This did not happen in the sermon, but in the after-meeting.
> And since then after-meetings have been used all over the
> country, and sinners are getting saved.

Franson saw all of this but he saw also the spiritual need
in the rural areas and up in the valleys of the country. He
announced two evangelist courses, April 3 and July 10, but
he expanded these to meet two particular needs and opportunities. He wrote:

> A Norwegian rural mission for the interior of Norway
> must be begun in which both men and women filled with the
> Holy Spirit may be used. In our day it is especially the youth
> whom the Lord is using, and not the least, the ladies. We
> seem to see Psalm 68:12 being fulfilled in our day, "The Lord

gives the command; the women who proclaim the good tidings are a great host" (so translated in several versions, including the New American Standard Bible).

Since the guitar has shown itself to be an effective means for drawing people to the meetings, the course also will offer instructions in guitar playing.

Some forty to fifty attended the first course, and of these, six men and fifteen women responded to the call to go out as missionaries to the remote areas of Norway. Unfortunately, shortly afterwards four of the men had to be withdrawn, but concerning all the others "the best of testimonies were given."

Fredrik Franson's First Finland Campaign

September 1 and 2, 1888 Franson shared in a holiness conference at Sunne in Värmland, Sweden and then moved on quickly to Finland, where, during the last week of September, he joined in meetings at Vasa with Constantin Boije, the pioneer evangelist of the Mission Covenant Church of Finland. The 60th Anniversary history of the Helsinki Free Church reported about Boije at this time: "During a visit to Sweden, where the Salvation Army had just begun work, he had become fascinated by its methods and believed for sure...that these methods had possibilities for great victories and gains in the Lord's cause," particularly in reaching the common masses. The Lord did indeed bless the joint meetings of Franson and Boije and many people were converted. But the meetings also caused a sensation. In Vasa, Tampere, Viborg, Helsinki, Åbo—yes, it seemed almost everywhere—the press reported with scorn on the smartly dressed young converts, ladies as well as men, who sang and gave testimonies (with small, red Bibles in their hands—like salvationists), or on the "Polynesian" type music, or the various recognizable personalities from the street culture as well as from Finland's elite society, that sometimes were featured in the meetings.

A meeting for students in the Helsinki University Music Hall drew an overflow crowd, including professors, some well known ladies, and Helsinki's bishop. Afterwards some 150 students went to the inquiry room. A three weeks' evangelist course began on November 6 with Franson's lectures being interpreted from Swedish into Finnish. One of the sixty some participants in this course was Hjalmar Braxén, an emerging leader of the Finnish free church movement. Another was Agnes Meyer, who in 1891 became Finland's first missionary to China serving with the Mission Covenant Church of Finland in association with the China Inland Mission. P. W. Lindahl gave this overview:

> The course received the very best reports. Several of the participants went out in two's all over the country as messengers of the Gospel. Some even went outside the borders to bring the salvation message to the people of Russia, and some reached even as far as Siberia.

> An official notice states, "Finland's people received great blessing from Franson's visit, particularly through the Bible and evangelist course that he conducted in the nation's capital."

During this time Franson was also making preparations for his projected campaign in Germany, but first he conducted an evangelist course in Örebro, Sweden, starting December 10, and then he also had an appointment in Oslo. The Örebro course drew some seventy to eighty participants. Thirty-five of these were commissioned at the end of the course as home missionaries. A number of these, particularly the ladies, were among the first evangelists of the newly formed Swedish Holiness Union ("Helgelseförbundet").

The East Africa Free Mission from Norway

Franson shared in a prophetic conference in Karlstad, Sweden January 12, 1889 with Pastor Ungerth of the Bethlehem Church. On the 14th he left for Oslo, Norway to take part in the commissioning service of Pastor Paul Wettergren from Arendal and his two sons for missionary service in Africa. He gave counsel and encouragement in their founding of the East Africa Free Mission, a mission which in 1899 was taken over by the Mission Covenant of Norway. On

February 6, Franson and the two Wettergren sons launched their deputation ministry in well attended meetings in Malmö, Sweden, and there Franson linked up with the man who was to become his most closely related associate and comrade in arms, Emanuel Olsson, a 28-year old evangelist of the Swedish Holiness Union. Emanuel Olsson was a postgraduate candidate from the Lund University. He had worked for some time in Michael Baxter's Gospel Union Mission in London and was planning to go to North Africa as a missionary. His father, a wealthy Christian businessman in Hälsingborg, was also the German consul in that city.

Franson's Third Germany Campaign

Franson and Emanuel Olsson arrived in Berlin in the middle of February 1889. Their plan was to develop a two-pronged campaign reaching the working masses in the various social democrat strongholds of Germany and also the students in seventeen university cities. Their first base in Berlin was the home of Pastor Weber from one of the state churches there. After a week of prayer they began an evangelist course on February 25 with some thirty to forty participants. They were soon holding evangelistic meetings in two different halls. Often the meetings were disturbed and police protection was offered, but souls were being saved. The Free Evangelical Missionary Association ("Freie evangelische Missions-Verein") was organized, and E. Krahn, a shoemaker, was elected chairman.

After the Berlin campaign Franson and Olsson worked separately in a long north-south stretch from the Hannover area to the Frankfurt area. Germany proved to be hard soil for them. Olsson, however, received some encouragement from Baptist groups. Franson also was encouraged in the university city of Göttingen where he had to extend his stay. Farther south he was pleased that the Hessen-Darmstadt church council made a church available to him for his meetings. Schools also were open to him. He found youth generally to be the most responsive. At the end of July he wrote:

We have already visited three universities, and God has been richly blessing. It has made an especially deep impression on them that we so strongly emphasize the great change that takes place in every person on his conversion. . . . After the messages, we give the students the opportunity to ask questions, and this has given us insight into the deeper questions of their hearts. . . . In every place we have had an opportunity to pray with some.

In this letter Franson also mentioned the alliance-minded revival periodical, *Gemeinschaftsblatt,* published by Anton Gerhard in Emden. It probably was during this period that Franson wrote the 16-page booklet, *Die edlen Söhne Zions und ihr Messias* (The Precious Sons of Zion and Their Messiah), which was published jointly by Gerhard in Emden and Carl Braus in Schwerte. Sometime during this period Mrs. Stjernwall from Helsinki also joined the work in Berlin.

In August there came a distinct change of pace for Franson. After four years of absence he returned to the Elberfeld-Barmen area for meetings and for ten days, when "a large host of sinners" turned to the Lord, he felt that an awakening was again taking place among the people. Forty to fifty turned to the Lord in September in the university city of Siegen. In October Franson was back in Berlin for meetings together with Emanuel Olsson. There were now forty members in the missionary association there. The young building inspector Beyerhaus had joined the group and was helping to provide indigenous leadership.

On November 5 Franson began a three-week evangelist course in Elberfeld, and he also had plans for a second evangelist course in Berlin beginning on December 27. During November two reinforcements arrived from Sweden, Richard Tjäder, a university student who spoke German, and a Brother Ullman.

The Founding of the German Alliance Mission

Toward the end of November 1889 Fredrik Franson wrote on a postcard from Barmen that some fifteen to thirty souls were seeking the Lord each night. In the evangelist course Franson had developed a new thrust. He wrote, "At least four brothers and two sisters from the evangelist course are heading for China. Student Tjäder these days is giving them a preparatory course in English." What was behind this new development? Kurt Zimmermann explains:

The Swedish evangelist Franson arrived in Barmen during this time. At one of the well known Neukirchen fall meetings in 1888 [this must have been in 1889], the decision was made through the influence of a burning message on China's need by Franson, to start a mission enterprise for China. Director Mandel and Carl Polnick—whose heart was aflame for this matter—then agreed among themselves that Polnick should handle this matter in Barmen.

Carl Polnick and Fredrik Franson had already taken the first decisive steps toward the founding of the German Alliance Mission early in November in connection with that evangelist course. The mission was named "Deutsche China-Allianz-Mission." Their step of faith received a significant vindication when the December 1889 issue of *China's Millions* arrived, carrying an editorial by Hudson Taylor entitled, "To Every Creature," here quoted:

If, in addition to the workers now in the field, one thousand whole-hearted evangelists, male and female, were set free and kept free for this special work, they might reach the whole number of China's millions before the end of 1895, and this allowing two years of the five for study of the language and preparation for the work. Estimating the population of China as we do at 250 million, there will be about 50 million of families; if fifty families were reached daily for 1,000 days by each of the 1,000 evangelists, every creature in China could be reached in three years' time, leaving the evangelist two or three Sundays for rest each month.

Also during this time, Fredrik Franson must have been concerned about the upcoming evangelist course in Berlin. On January 16, 1890, a day or two before the course came to an end, four new reinforcements arrived from Sweden. They were Emil Jakobson, the two lady evangelists, Nelly Hall and Ninnie Åkeson, and the singer Ida Nihlen. A new evangelistic thrust in Berlin was then launched. The opposition on the north side of the city was still vehement. However, souls were being saved in the mission association's regular meeting place. Soon the membership increased to about fifty.

In the middle of February, Richard Tjäder was put in charge of the Berlin work. Ninnie Åkeson went to Wiesbaden to help in the work of Count Modest M. Korff, and Emanuel Olsson, Nelly Hall, and Ida Nihlen joined Franson in the Barmen area.

Opposition in Barmen, too, was strong, but the number of new converts throughout the area increased to around five hundred. The churches generally did not favor the movement, so Franson worked with some of the local leaders, including Polnick of Barmen and Reismann of Elberfeld, to organize the Alliance Missionary Association ("Alianz-Missions-Verein") which soon had over 200 members. One reason for the clergy's opposition apparently was Franson's use of women on his team, as well as what seemed to them to be his Salvation Army-like methods generally. Therefore, as he had done once before in the case of the after-meetings, he now prepared a thorough study of the biblical basis for women's participation in evangelism. The result was a 40-page booklet, *Weissagende Töchter* (Prophesying Daughters), which also was published in issues Nos. 16 and 17 of *Gemeinschaftsblatt*. Later that year a Norwegian translation also appeared.

Deputation Ministry for the China Mission

The main preoccupation of both Franson and the local leaders at this time was the mission to China. The volunteers for China as well as other participants in the November evangelist course were busy in evangelism throughout the Ruhr area. Reports of souls being saved came in from many communities. At the same time through the pages of *Gemeinschaftsblatt* Franson and the committee members kept the interested constituency informed of the progress of their planning and arrangements as well as the various cost estimates. Franson in particular emphasized how individuals and groups might share in the support of a specific missionary on a regular basis. Funds and donations in kind began to come in. Franson himself at this time received an inheritance from his mother, and he contributed half (2,500 marks) to the transportation fund for the outgoing missionaries. Finally, the team of volunteers, four men and three women, set out with Franson and Olsson on a farewell tour that included the Ruhr, the Bonn, and the Frankfurt areas. Correspondence with the China Inland Mission resulted in the offer of an associate arrangement that the German Alliance Mission accepted. After a blessed meeting in Barmen on Pentecost Sunday the group set off for London, England, where the volunteers were to be a part of China Inland Mission's candidate program for a few months before final acceptance and departure for the field.

While in London, Franson wrote on June 9 to his friends in the United States that he believed the Lord wanted him to accept their invitations to come back to America for evangelistic work there. He planned tentatively to spend two years in America, one year working among the Scandinavians and one among the Germans.

Later in the fall of 1890 Emanuel Olsson returned to Germany and reported on meetings in Berlin and Wiesbaden and in East Prussia. Several additional volunteers for China came out of these meetings. During Olsson's visit in Wiesbaden an "Allianz-Missions-Verein" was organized on the pattern of the one in Barmen, this only shortly before Count Korff, a member of the Mission's Barmen committee, was leaving for Neuchatel, Switzerland.

The Roots of the Swiss Alliance Mission

By then three candidates had been finally selected for the first party to leave for China, Joseph Bender and the Misses Elizabeth Bäumer and Auguste Schnütgen. The final series of farewell meetings for them was scheduled to begin in Barmen on October 5. Emanuel Olsson was to travel with them. Their itinerary included Barmen, Hagen, Schwelm, Haspe, Soest, Nümbrecht, Siegen, Wiesbaden, Frankfurt, Dinglingen, Baden, Stuttgart, Basel, Zürich, with final departure by

boat from Genoa on October 27. In the meantime, Carl Polnick had written to a like-minded businessman in Zürich,
Hermann Scholder-Develay, and this brother received the
group and arranged for their meetings in Switzerland. Interest and involvement were born that soon spread to other
Swiss brethren as well. Before long a home committee for
the Allianz-China-Mission was set up in Switzerland. This
eventually became the Swiss Alliance Mission ("Schweizer
Allianz Mission") of today.

3

FREDRIK FRANSON AND MISSIONARY EXTENSION
INTO ALL THE WORLD

Fredrik Franson at this point was thirty-eight years old.
He had already begun on the third and last major phase of
his life's work, that of encouraging and organizing missionary extension into all the world. This phase includes three
distinct periods: 1) the TEAM and C&MA period, 1890-1897;
2) the Heavenly Timeclock *(Himlauret)* period, 1897-1902;
and 3) the period of the practical global missiologist and revival nurturer, 1902-1908.

The Beginning of TEAM

Fredrik Franson arrived in New York on Sunday, September 7, 1890, and spoke in four different churches that day.
For the next five weeks he had almost daily meetings in the
New York metropolitan and New England areas. On September 16 he began announcing an evangelist course to be
held in the Pilgrim Church, Brooklyn, beginning October 14.
The announcement included the following information:

> Brothers and sisters from any Christian denomination,
> who have a burning desire to use their time and strength to
> bring the Gospel to the millions in their own and other coun-
> tries hastening toward perdition, and who wish to study the
> Bible in order to equip themselves for such a task, are heart-
> ily welcome. Over a dozen such courses have been held in

the last years in several countries, such as Sweden, Norway, Finland, and Germany, and have proven to be, despite the brevity, of great blessing, and many of the participants have later gone with the Good News to different countries of Europe, as well as China and Africa.

Some fifty persons attended this course. About twenty volunteered for the mission to China. Franson's aim was to have an "expedition" ready to leave for China at the end of January 1891.

On November 4, Franson announced an 11-day evangelist course for Chicago, beginning November 25, and similar courses for Minneapolis on December 30, and Omaha on January 13. He also published in *Chicago-Bladet* on November 25, 1890, an article entitled, "China's Millions," in which he outlined the foundational principles and approaches of the Alliance Mission from America that he had in mind. Its first task was to function within the scope of Hudson Taylor's editorial, which called for one thousand evangelists to concentrate on the evangelization of China within three years, and for that purpose these missionaries were to function mainly as itinerant missionaries for the first three years under the general leadership of Hudson Taylor. At the same time, each missionary was to stand in a responsible relationship to his supporting churches and, after the three-year period, in consultation with these supporting churches, to be free to transfer to some other board should that be desired. As had previously been practiced in the evangelist courses in Europe, the last day of each course was to be set aside for fasting and prayer. Franson appealed to all the Lord's people among the Scandinavians in North America to set aside December 5 and January 9, the last days of the Chicago and Minneapolis courses, to join with the course participants in fasting and prayer for the future of this itinerant evangelistic mission in China.

A medical Samaritan course was announced for Omaha beginning January 5, 1891 to which all the volunteers for China were directed to come. Well over 170 persons had attended the first three evangelist courses. From among the China volunteers that came to the Omaha Samaritan course thirty-five were selected for the first expedition to leave Omaha on January 17 and fifteen for the second expedition to leave on January 29.

The Omaha evangelist course got under way January 19 with some seventy participants. The fifth course commenced in Lindsborg, Kansas on February 9. Five more courses were conducted in the latter half of 1891 in Seattle, Washington; Denver, Colorado; Phelps Center, Nebraska; Des Moines, Iowa; and Chicago.

A group of fifteen missionaries was sent to Japan, leaving on November 1891. A third party with twelve left for China on February 14, 1892. On March 9, ten missionaries with John F. Fredrickson as leader left for the Himalaya region, and on April 2 eight missionaries embarked for South Africa. During this one and a half year period after the beginning of the first evangelist course in Brooklyn, Franson had had much administrativo oorroopondonoo and arrangements to handle in connection with these outgoing parties of missionaries. To share responsibility and handle the home affairs of the new mission he had, by the end of the Chicago course, called together five very capable and representative Scandinavian men in the Chicago area. By January 1891 this committee was functioning. This committee then became the basis of the Allianco Mission, soon to be officially named "The Scandinavian Alliance Mission of North America." Tho namo was changed to Tho Evangelical Alliance Mission (TEAM) in 1949.

On April 4, 1892, Fredrik Franson could write:

The Alliance Mission now has 59 missionaries in China proper, 14 in Japan, 10 on the way to Tibet, and 8 on the way to Africa, a total of 91. May God bless all of them richly! Dear friends, continue to pray much for our missionaries, because they need it. Pray also for me, that my projected tent campaign among the Norwegians in the great Norwegian settlements this spring, and into the summer, may be of great blessing.

The Two Hundred for C&MA's "Swedish Field" in China

The April 22, 1892 issue of *The Christian Alliance and*

Missionary Work contained the following excerpt from the report of the General Secretary and Superintendent A. B. Simpson of the International Missionary Alliance (now C&MA) for the month ended April 9, 1892:

> A very remarkable movement has been pressed upon us by the Spirit and providence of God...represented by the Rev. Mr. Franson, a devoted evangelist and missionary, offering to the Board, without any expense whatever for all the preliminary training required, two hundred of the most consecrated workers of Sweden, especially trained for missionary service in China, with the pledge that they will undertake to live in that field on the small sum of two hundred dollars per year, and that the expense of sending them to their field will not greatly exceed one hundred dollars each. Very thorough inquiry has been made into this matter.
>
> Mr. Franson has already met with the Board in personal conference....Can it be that the Master is opening another door for the supply of missionaries for our China work, and that He would have us very prayerfully and courageously consider this call, and be very sure before we decline it?

The June 30, 1892 issue of *Missionæren* contains the full text of a letter written by Franson at the end of May in which he also told about this undertaking. Under the heading, "CONSECRATE YOURSELVES: For Tomorrow the Lord Will Do Amazing Things Among You" (Joshua 3:5), Franson explained how, when he arrived in New York in 1890, he had met A. B. Simpson who also had started an alliance mission, how this last winter he had met him again in Omaha, how this particular proposal then had been developed between them, and about the prayer that had followed it ever since, especially after a first letter from A. B. Simpson expressing tentative interest. Franson then continues:

> A week ago Saturday, I got a letter from New York with the decisive answer from Brother Simpson and the friends in his mission. After much consideration and prayer, they had decided to accept my proposal. Had they not done that, then I probably would be on my way to Japan, China, etc. this fall, but that trip will now be postponed at least for the time being.
>
> My decision is to leave for Sweden now and to conduct evangelist courses for volunteers for this service, make ar-

rangements for their travel; and God will show whom He wants to go, be it more or less than 200.

Franson left New York July 9, 1892 for Sweden on this undertaking which would occupy him fully for the next year and a half. In the next twelve months more than five hundred persons attended his evangelist courses in Sweden and Norway, and of these he selected two hundred as the candidates for the projected C&MA "Swedish Field" in China. He followed the plan and procedures worked out with the C&MA in New York. The first forty-five of these missionaries had arrived in China in two separate parties by the spring of 1893. A. B. Simpson, who was in China at this time, selected Franson's co-worker of the Germany campaign, Emanuel Olsson, as the Superintendent of this Swedish Field. Some of the TEAM missionaries were asked to help with the language studies. These C&MA Swedish missionaries were assigned a field in North China, north of the Great Wall, and they gradually opened stations from Kalgan to Ningsia. In the meantime, the preparations for sending out the other 155 of these missionary candidates from Sweden were halted by a cablegram from New York, giving the reason as financial difficulties.

Franson was able to hold the candidates together until the fall, arranging English language instruction for them and sending them out in evangelism, but when the funds then still had not come, he had to release them. He was able to help many of them find other avenues of effective service. A few found their way to the States and were accepted by the C&MA there. However, at the end of 1893, there still were fifty of them in Sweden, holding out for service in China with the C&MA. The C&MA finally selected sixteen of them during 1894, and they were sent to the field in 1895.

Franson's Missionary Observation and Evaluation Tour

Fredrik Franson left Malmö, Sweden January 5, 1894 setting out on his first overseas missionary observation tour. He went first through Germany and Switzerland, eastern Europe and Palestine, and then by ship from Cairo to India.

In Cairo he learned of the Homecall of Emanuel Olsson. In India, Franson first visited the fields of several other missions, including the C&MA, the Swedish Evangelical National Foundation, and the Santal Mission. Finally in April he arrived in the Darjeeling-Ghoom area where he met John F. Fredrickson and the other missionaries on TEAM's Himalaya Field.

Franson worked with his fellow missionaries in the Himalaya region for five months. On one trip he traveled with two of the missionaries to the western Tibet region, in the mountains up from Mussoorie, where he helped those two missionaries open a new station in the Tibetan border town of Nilang. In the same way in which he had studied Mormonism in Utah fifteen years earlier, Franson now studied the Buddhism of Tibet and wrote a 48-page booklet, *The Religion of Tibet and True Religion: For English-speaking Tibetans.* This book soon was translated into Tibetan to be sent with travelers into Tibet. Altogether he wrote eight different tracts for the Tibetan work.

By mid-October Franson had reached Canton, South China, where he visited the work of the Evangelical Free Church of America, which at that time was supervised by Alfred Alf. He then went on to Japan where he spent the months of November and December. He was deeply warmed and moved by the work of his fellow missionaries here. They had arranged that he conduct an evangelist course in Tokyo for their Japanese fellow workers, and after this, while these workers carried on the work at the stations, Franson and several of the missionaries made a more thorough survey of the needs and opportunities in Japan. This then became the basis of the further development of their work.

Franson spent January through July, 1895 in China. He had several conferences with Hudson Taylor during this period; he visited the German Alliance Mission field in southern Chekiang and met with its eight missionaries; he had a five-day conference at Yüshan, Kiangsi, attended by eleven TEAM missionaries, four of the Germans, and four others from the CIM; he met with some thirty C&MA missionaries, including 15 Scandinavians, at a conference in Wuhu on the Yangtze River; in North China, he visited a number of the American Board missionaries, and conferred with the forty-five missionaries on C&MA's Swedish Field north of the Great Wall, as well as with the three Swedish Holiness missionaries who worked between the two branches of the Wall in northern Shansi; then he also consulted with Erik Folke and the other Swedish Mission in China missionaries in southern Shansi. In each place he had preaching ministries.

Of TEAM's fifty-five missionaries in China at this time, forty-two had been relocated from their former CIM stations to a field of their own on the Sian plain in Shensi Province and also up into Kansu Province. Towards the end of May Franson joined in a conference with all of these missionaries and then visited their work at seven of the eight stations they had opened so far. He found that they had developed an effective work with eight different types of ministry. He recognized, however, their need for a printing press and arranged to secure one for them in Japan.

On his way back to Shanghai, Franson again stopped by the stations of some other missions including the Norwegian Lutherans at Laohoko, both the American and the Swedish Covenant missions and the Norwegian-American Lutherans. He then had a three week stopover in Japan, before arriving back in North America on September 4, 1895. He had seen the work of many missions from India to Japan, including that of almost all of the so-called "Franson missionaries," and what he had seen of their work had not been a disappointment.

Ministering at the Home Base

Fredrik Franson came back from North China with a great burden to get work started among the Mongols. To his great joy, almost at once David Stenberg, a seminary graduate, offered himself and was sent out before the end of 1895. At the beginning of January 1896, Franson attended the annual meeting of the TEAM Committee, to which the treasurers of the supporting churches also were invited. During its first five years, the mission had had a commendably low attrition rate. At the end of that first special three-year period, a few of the missionaries had transferred through marriage to other missions, but few had changed mission status for other reasons. The Lord had called several home to Himself through sickness, and some had had to return home because of continuing health problems. It became clear, however, that now more official information was needed at home about the mission's work. So in May, Fredrik Franson published an article in which he brought the work statistics of the mission up to date. In this article he also made clear that the general ongoing policy of the mission was more than evangelism alone; the mission also stressed church development. Some missionaries concentrated on evangelism, others on church development. Franson explained:

> The Alliance Mission establishes stations and strives toward the establishment of Christian congregations. . . . It was quite interesting to me to observe that many of the missionaries who here at home had developed mostly the evangelist's gift, on the field also had developed to quite an extent shepherding, teaching, and leadership gifts.

A second seminary graduate, Carl Suber, in the summer of 1896, offered himself for Mongolia, and before the end of the year, he too was on his way out.

In December 1896, Fredrik Franson again met with the TEAM Committee. The decision was taken to incorporate the mission in Illinois. A subcommittee was appointed to work with Franson in developing a proposed constitutional draft, and on the basis of this draft the mission was incorporated in November 1897. Franson now was officially appointed General Director.

During this time in North America, Franson was deeply burdened about certain other matters also. He held consistently and without reservation to the futurist interpretation of Revelation. However, he was not willing to exclude all value from the historicist interpretation. He saw no serious conflict between all the then converging historicist pointers

to a rapidly approaching end of the age and "millennial sab-
bath," and the futurist any-moment expectation of Christ's
return that he held to be the only lasting biblical position. To
him the significant point was that from both the historicist
and the futurist perspective the return of Christ was now
imminent.

To Franson this had some serious implications. Because
the Church is one in Christ, and in the most real sense will
be so in the rapture, barriers that separate brethren and
distract from our oneness in Christ ought not to be and
should be removed if possible. Franson saw a particular
need and a ripening opportunity in this direction in the three
church groupings, Covenant, Congregational, and Free
Church, that had emerged from the Swedish Lutheran pietist movement in America. He therefore proposed that each
of these three groups should consider rejoining the two
others. The groups responded tentatively and for several
years each maintained a committee to probe this possibility.
But in the end nothing more came of the effort.

Another concern of Franson's at this time, however,
brought more lasting results. In his itinerating around the
country Franson had observed many pastorless Scandinavian congregations served by one or two of the local
laymen. Many of these men had expressed to him their need
for more training in the Bible for the demanding work committed to them, but they had little opportunity for regular
training. Franson, therefore, announced two evangelist
courses, one in Oakland, Nebraska, beginning September
29, 1896 and one at Christine, North Dakota, beginning October 27, in which matters relating to the work of the elder
were to be given special attention. As a result of these
courses four regional associations for pastors, elders, and
evangelists were organized—one for Nebraska, another for
North Dakota and Western Minnesota, one for Illinois, and
one for the Norwegians in Southern Minnesota. The Minis-
terial Association of the Evangelical Free Church of America in its early years partially built on these foundations.

In the spring of 1897 Franson conducted evangelist

courses in the eastern United States. The last one was at Worcester, Massachusetts, designed particularly for volunteers for Mongolia. From that group five were accepted. When Franson left for Europe on June 9, 1897 he could report that during the previous six years a total of 125 missionaries had been sent to the fields through TEAM. Of these, one hundred were still in active service overseas, 87 in TEAM and 13 with other missions. Including the five new missionaries for Mongolia, TEAM's new total would be 92 missionaries.

The Founding of the Swedish Mongol Mission

When Fredrik Franson landed in Oslo, June 21, 1897 he began what might be called the "heavenly timeclock" period in his life. He had many well attended meetings in both Norway and Sweden as well as a number of evangelist courses, but his real preoccupation all fall was the writing of the book, *Himlauret* (The Heavenly Timeclock). As far back as the spring of 1886 Franson had worked out an ingenious system of chronology for the time before the resurrection of Christ's body, the Church, based on an analogy of the time between Christ's suffering on the cross and his third-day resurrection from the dead. In *Himlauret* he applies this chronological system to both the 2,500 *years* of "the times of the gentiles" to give a *historicist* perspective of Revelation, and also to the 2,500 *days* of judgment to give a *futurist* perspective of Revelation. The book was published in Stockholm in November 1897.

Yet in his public meetings during this time Franson's call to missions was as strong as ever. After hearing his description of the Mongols a young engineer and his wife in Sweden volunteered for missionary service among the Mongols. To help them, Franson telegraphed to the chairwoman of the YWCA in Stockholm with the result that a meeting was arranged there for October 4. That meeting was the beginning of the Swedish Mongol Mission ("Svenska Mongolmissionen"), today called the Swedish East Asia Mission after having merged with the Swedish Mission in China. Prince

Bernadotte, brother of the King, served as the mission's first chairman. The young engineer and his wife left for Mongolia in the spring of 1898.

The Founding of the Finnish Alliance Mission

Franson arrived in Barmen, Germany on New Year's Eve and began meetings throughout the area, which resulted in great blessing. About 130 attended the evangelist course that began at the end of January 1898. *Die Himmelsuhr*, the German edition of *Himlauret*, came off the press later in the spring.

Franson then moved on to a ministry in Silesia and then into Russia and up through the Baltic states. The Helsinki Free Church had asked him to return, and he worked his way gradually up to Finland. In many places along the way large numbers turned to the Lord. Franson began his ministry in Finland on March 28, 1898 at Viborg. From Easter Sunday through April 19 he was in Helsinki where he helped found a Finnish mission to Bulgaria. Cash contributions as well as quarterly subscriptions were received, and a committee was to be formed. Franson also at this time helped organize the Finnish Alliance Mission as the Finnish Department of TEAM. By the fall of 1898 this mission had sent out its first missionaries to the Himalaya region, Brother and Sister K. Waismaa and the Misses Hilja Heiskanen and A. Massinen. Also in the fall of 1898, *Taiwaan kello*, the Finnish edition of *Himlauret*, was published.

In 1906, when TEAM opened its Western India Field among the Bhil people, all of its Himalaya work was turned over to the Finnish Alliance Mission, and that mission in 1910 merged with the Finnish Free Church ("Suomen Vapaakirkon") since it represented exactly the same home constituency in Finland.

Toward the Founding of a Sisters Home for Evangelism in Borken, West Prussia

During the summer of 1898 Franson was busy in a writing

ministry in Norway. In the fall he returned to Finland and
Russia, going on from there into Germany from where he
wrote:

It is with the greatest gratitude to God that I want to
describe in a few words the changes that seem to have taken
place for the better here in Germany in the last few years, at
least as far as the Gospel is concerned.

Shortly after arriving here in northern Germany, I was invited by two believing Lutheran pastors to conduct evangelistic services with after-meetings in the churches they were
serving. . . .

Among those who attended these evangelistic services
was a Col. von Schmeling. . . who together with some believing Lutheran pastors invited me to a large evangelical conference in the well-known city of Königsberg, East Prussia.

The conference took place November 8–11, 1898. One of
the pastors on the sponsoring committee was Ferdinand Blazejewski of Borken. Here is an excerpt from *Evangelische
Allianz-Blatt's* report on that conference:

It was a joy to hear pastors of the State Church conduct
such evangelistic services with after-meetings in which
everyone who wanted to come to Christ was exhorted to
stand up, take a seat in front, and pray aloud on their own.
In the two evenings, there must have been at least fifty who
found peace. Hallelujah! Honor be to the Lord!

During the period immediately preceding, a number of
state church pastors in both Pomerania and Prussia had
been converted, and a wonderful new revival wind was
blowing through the whole region. To help bring the Gospel
to the many rural hamlets in the area at this time, Franson
arranged a Bible course at Graudenz beginning December
27. Sixteen men and women attended. Franson rejoiced that
several believing pastors worked together in an effort to
give the revival some organization to keep it going in unity
and strength. He was particularly happy because five of
these pastors had formed a committee to found and operate
a home for women evangelists, the "Gemeinschaftsschwest-
ernhaus" in Borken and its related sponsoring association,
the "Gemeinschafts-Schwestern-Verband."

August Kmitta, the Chrischona missionary who then was

in charge of the Pilgrim Mission's Elbing work, wrote about Franson's ministry during this time:

> In the meantime the Lord had laid on his heart the organization of the revival fellowships. Few know today that Franson is the father of our fellowship statutes....Often we sat consulting with him till deep in the night. A number of clauses were written out by hand, printed, and according to them the Elbing Fellowship was organized. A large number of revival fellowships in West and East Prussia were later organized according to these by-laws....Just think, for instance, how wise his basic clause was that a local congregation under the Spirit is both the highest authority, and that the only way outside individuals or fellowships can serve it is through brotherly counsel.
>
> But we could open ourselves less up to his idea of sending out as many women evangelists as possible....But all the more willing were those recently converted pastors to take up these ideas of Franson's, among them the beloved Pastor Blazejewski in Borken, who has since been called home to the Lord. He opened up his parsonage for the training of ladies, first of all to become evangelists. It is from this beginning that the Vandsburg Sisters Home has developed.

Pastor Paul Fabianke from the "Kinderheil" work also reported on these developments: "In any case, Franson's plea for women in the ministry of the Word was not without fruit. Pastor Blazejewski in Borken, who was converted in 1892, a fiery person full of zeal and love for his Savior, was a somewhat kindred spirit to Franson. He took up his cause and set it before both God and the brethren, and in 1899 he founded the Fellowship Sisters Home ("Gemeinschafts-schwesternhaus") by receiving converted young women into his parsonage for training as evangelists."

The sisters home at Borken was opened on October 20, 1899 with four trainees. Pastor Blazejewski had carefully worked out the principles and the course of studies to be followed. His key point: "The sisters are first of all to be trained in soul winning and spiritual counseling. In the light of this, the training for and practice in nursing care will be kept secondary." A few months later, on May 24, 1900, the Lord called the 39-year old Blazejewski home to Himself. However, the seed sown had sprouted. The home was taken

over by one of the other pastors on the committee, Theophil
Krawielitzki, and he moved it to Vandsburg. Today this
seedling has become the huge tree we know as "Deutsche
Gemeinschafts-Diakonieverband" (the German Fellowship
Deaconry Union) with its own foreign missionary arm, the
Marburg Mission.

The Founding of the Swedish Alliance Mission

After these blessings in Germany, Franson returned to
Sweden rejoicing. His joy was tempered, however, by news
awaiting him there. It had become clear that serious financial difficulties were besetting some of the missionaries on
the C&MA Swedish Field, and a number had even left the
field. An appeal had been sent to some of the missions in
Sweden, and at least one of these, the Jönköping Missionary
Association, had sent out some emergency funds. All of this
troubled Franson deeply. Again he felt the burden of Sweden's uncompleted missionary commitment to China, and so
in a quiet way he began again to share the burden. One by
one some six to eight young people volunteered, and faith
promises came in for their support. Franson approached
several missions about taking on the administration of this
project, but none was willing. China was in a time of in-
creasing unrest, and none could think about opening a new
field there at such a time.

Franson was encouraged, however, to approach the Jönköping Missionary Association. Its Board in February 1900
gave approval to the project, adopted an enabling recommendation to its Annual Conference and even appointed a
committee of five men to handle the whole arrangement.
Other factors then came in, and in March the Board re-
scinded its recommendation. Two months passed. The members of the association, however, made it clear at this time
that they wanted to become involved in a mission of their
own. Finally, four of the men on the committee, together
with a fifth brother, on March 25, 1900, met with Franson,
and after a memorable season of prayer these five men con-
stituted themselves as "the committee for the Swedish

Department of the Scandinavian Alliance Mission." In 1913 they changed the name to the Swedish Alliance Mission ("Svenska Alliansmissionen"). Its first two missionaries to India arrived in 1900, the first missionary to South Africa in 1901, and its first seven missionaries to China reached there in 1902.

The Closing of C&MA's Swedish Field and the Opening of SAM's China Field

In June 1900 the Boxer hordes in China were unleashed and massacres began. The casualties were staggering. No one knows how many Chinese Christians were murdered. The total among the missionaries was 135, plus 51 children. For the Franson-related missions the blow was indeed heavy. The C&MA Swedish Field lost twenty-one of its thirty-two missionaries on the field. Ten Swedish Holiness Mission personnel were killed. Five of TEAM's six Mongolia Field missionaries were also martyred. The Swedish Mongol Mission lost its three missionaries.

There is an interesting sequel to this sad story. The C&MA's Swedish Field had been blotted out of existence, but seven of its eleven survivors wanted to go back. In 1901 these seven came as a group to the Swedish Alliance Mission's annual conference and asked to be taken on as missionaries for its projected China Field. They were accepted, and before the end of 1902 they were back north of the Great Wall, opening the Swedish Alliance Mission's new China Field.

The Beginning of the Norwegian Missionary Alliance

Another story centers around Ludvig Eriksen, the only Norwegian on the C&MA Swedish Field. He and Franson had first worked together in Norway during the summer of 1890. When Franson arrived in Shanghai in 1895 Ludvig Eriksen was there to meet him. Eriksen was stationed for a number of years farther northwest in Ningsia, but some time before 1900 he moved to Peking. From there he carried on an extensive itineration ministry, working among both

Chinese and Mongols north of the Great Wall, especially ex-
tending his work through Chinese evangelists whom he
trained. But weakened in health he returned to Norway in
the spring of 1900. After the Boxer Uprising he discovered
that all but one of his Chinese fellow evangelists had been
massacred. He then gave himself to developing a new mission that would again take up the training and sending out of
national evangelists in North China, and thus the Norwegian
Missionary Alliance ("Norsk Misjonsallianse") had its
beginning. For years the field supervision of that mission
was carried on by Carl Söderbom, one of the seven ex-
C&MA Swedes who had gone back to China with the Swedish Alliance Mission. In 1910 the Norwegian Missionary Alliance sent out its own first missionary to China.

Franson's Unsuccessful Effort to Visit South Africa

After the Swedish Alliance Mission Jönköping Committee
had been established in May 1900, Fredrik Franson went to
Holland, Portugal, and Spain for ministries and then started
out on a trip that he hoped would take him overland through
the Sahara and down to the TEAM field in South Africa.
However, because of the continuing Boer War there, it
became necessary for him to change his plans while still in
North Africa. He travelled instead to Greece, Bulgaria
(where he noted that now he had preached the Gospel in
every country of Europe), southern Russia, and finally again
to Finland. He was in the middle of an evangelist course in
Helsinki when, on July 22, 1901 a party of Swedish survivors
from the Boxer massacres in North China came through.
They had spent a full year on the trip, crossing both
Mongolia and Siberia before reaching European Russia.

Returning to the United States

Shortly thereafter Franson returned to the United States
disembarking at Boston on September 19. That whole fall he
was busy evangelizing among Jews and Germans on the East
Coast. In March 1902 he was again in Chicago, and in July in
Phelps Center, Nebraska. On August 14, 1902 he left San

Francisco by ship on a work and study mission that over a period of six years would take him to mission fields throughout the Pacific, East, South, and West Asia, East and South Africa, and Latin America.

Fredrik Franson's Final Six years of Revival Ministries and Missiological Studies

Franson made stops in the Fiji Islands, New Zealand (where he helped organize two Scandinavian local churches), Australia (where he launched a Scandinavian Seaman's Mission), the Philippines, and arrived in Hong Kong on Christmas Eve. For the first two and a half months of 1903 he visited and conducted meetings in Canton and in several provinces along the way to Shanghai (where he also launched a Scandinavian Seaman's Mission). In Wenchow fifteen to twenty souls sought the Lord each night. Everywhoro ho oboorvod tho work, moanwhilo working with thc missionaries, questioning and consulting with them concerning the best way to nurture the believers. He then went on to Japan where he worked with great blessing for seven months. In October 1903 he was in Korea where his ministry in Wonson led to one of the crucial victories in the early days of the Korea revival. In November he was used of the Lord in a revival ministry among the students in CIM's Chefoo Schools for missionary children. He moved into Manchuria, back down to Ticntsin, and finally arrived on the Swedish Alliance Mission's China Field north of the Great Wall in mid-December.

The Third Year: China

Fredrik Franson then spent nine months working with the missionaries in the interior of North China (including Inner Mongolia), the Northwest, and West China until he arrived in Chengtu. From there he followed the Yangtze River, stopping in several places along the way, until he reached Shanghai. From there he took a boat to Foochow where the Lord again blessed with a revival ministry. By Christmas 1904 he had traveled as far as Burma.

The Fourth Year: South Asia

During February and March 1905 Franson worked with his fellow missionaries on the Himalaya Field. He also visited the new SAM and TEAM fields among the Bhil people in Western India, and then in the fall he moved into the Kashmir where TEAM had a work in Baltistan. During these months in India several hundred persons came to faith in Christ through Franson's ministry.

January through March 1906: The Armenian Revival

Franson next traveled to Karachi and across to the Persian Gulf and up to Baghdad. From Baghdad he took a 20-day trip north to Urmia in Iran and then over to Van in Eastern Turkey where he preached to 5,000 Armenians. He moved on westward and finally arrived in Diyarbekir shortly before Christmas 1905. He moved on to Harpoot where Dr. Atkinson of the American Board was waiting for him. Franson now entered into another evangelistic ministry through which the awakening waves again moved among the Armenian people. The Armenian preacher Apraham Hoja Levonian was strongly influenced by Franson at this time, and many of the youth that were saved then became leaders of the dispersed Armenian spiritual movement right on into the post-World War II period.

Two Years in Africa and in South America

It was in April 1906 that Franson left Beirut for Uganda and then on to South Africa, where, after working for several months with his own fellow Scandinavian missionaries (TEAM, SAM, and Holiness), he moved into a year-long ministry among the Dutch Boers during which time he had close fellowship with Pastor Andrew Murray. In one of his campaigns at that time five hundred were saved in a ten-day period. An evangelist course was conducted at Robinson in June 1907 with over two hundred participants.

Franson left South Africa for Argentina and Brazil in August 1907. In Porto Alegro, Brazil a mission hall was opened for the German Revival Fellowship. His visit to some Swedish settlements in the interior led to the Örebro Mission's taking up work there. Franson then crossed over the Andes and stopped for ministries in Chile, Peru, and Panama. He then proceeded to Maracaibo, Venezuela, where two TEAM missionaries, T. J. Bach and John Christiansen, had recently begun Gospel work with a varied approach that included both literature and boat ministries.

The Caribbean and Mexico—Fredrik Franson's Last Manuscript

Franson also visited several of the Caribbean islands where again the Lord's blessing required that he stay longer than planned. During May 1908 he was in Mexico. It was there that he completed the manuscript, "Missionary Methods on the Foreign Field," which he had begun in Africa. In it he discussed five methods of missionary work: 1) the ritualistic child-rearing method; 2) the exclusive pure-church method; 3) the philanthropic or indirect method; 4) the exclusive direct evangelization method (the Nevius Method as applied in Korea); and 5) the mass baptism method (simple disciple making combined with people movement dynamics). He sent the manuscript to his good friend pharmacist Efraim Sandblom in Jönköping. On June 5 he crossed the border into the United States; and on July 3 he moved into a small house in Idaho Springs, Colorado for a month of rest. There on August 2, 1908, the Lord called Fredrik Franson home to Himself. He was 56 years old.

Franson's last manuscript, with an introduction by Sandblom, was published in Jönköping in 1909 in the 60-page book, *Missionär F. Fransons Testamente: Fem olika missionsmetoder* (Missionary F. Franson's Testament: Five Different Methods of Missionary Work).

EPILOGUE

The foregoing presents only a bare outline of Fredrik Franson's extremely full life and fruitful ministry. The words of the Lord Jesus about John the Baptist can surely be applied: "He was a burning and a shining light" (John 5:35). For a third of a century Franson's zeal for lost men, women, and children never slackened. Church history has the record of some remarkably dedicated men whose ministry blessed multitudes. Surely among them must be numbered this man who labored with such outstanding devotion and faithfulness.

The principles set down by Jesus seemed to some to have contradictions, "He that findeth his life shall lose it; and he that loseth his life for my sake shall find it" (Matthew 10:39). Franson's life can best be understood in the light of that principle. He was personally unaffected, simple, and self-effacing and yet, at the same time, forward, forceful, and tenaciously persuasive in ministry. His personal possessions were meager, yet he could appeal for large sums of money for the Lord's work. His roots were in a mining community in Sweden and in the raw American frontier; yet he was more advanced, forward looking, and intellectually astute than many with greater privileges. He preached a simple message but dug deeply into the Word of God to undergird his presentations with a solid scriptural foundation.

His evangelistic campaigns had no advance men, no pub-

91

lic relations department, no administrative structure, but
for over thirty years Franson was active in long evangelistic
campaigns, following one upon another, that reached thousands in each place and reaped hundreds of souls in most.

His influence did not depend on organizational position.
He held office in one church organization briefly at age 23
and for twelve years was General Director of TEAM (though
without an office or a desk), and yet his vision, principles of
organization, and spiritual leadership resulted in the founding of stable mission societies and church fellowships in
many parts of the world.

At the time, the work he began seemed to have poor pros-
pects for continued success considering the lack of formally
organized headquarters, the modest financing, and the lack
of academic preparation on the part of some of his missionaries. But these ministries have survived and flourished. In
some way, Franson was able to choose workers and associ-
ates in ministry who shared his vision and absorbed his
scriptural principles of action. His influence is still strong in
these ministries today yet at times without a conscious
realization of the source of the example followed.

There is another personal factor that must be considered
in Franson's life as a key to his effectiveness. Without it his
life, his work, and his influence defy explanation. It is that
which he gave as a theme to so many of his training courses
and sought more than anything else to inculcate into the
thousands of students who took these courses and then scattered to reap the ripening harvest fields. It was epitomized
in his oft-repeated expression: CONSTANT CONSCIOUS COM-
MUNION WITH CHRIST. In a word, it was the Spirit-filled life
that ever kept Christ central.

But along with this key Fredrik Franson also was recep-
tive to the help and contributions of others, and he dedicated his natural, developed, and given gifts 100% to God's
service in the bringing of men and women around the world
to the assurance of salvation. To his life there is no problem
applying the words of the apostle Paul in I Corinthians
15:10:

But by the grace of God I am what I am, and his grace to me was not without effect. No, I worked harder than all of them—yet not I, but the grace of God that was with me.

This is the heritage of all who follow in the footsteps of Fredrik Franson—of those in the missions and fellowships that his vision, obedience, and fervor brought into being and fruitfulness.

Appendix I

Mission Societies and Church Fellowships Founded or Strongly Influenced by Fredrik Franson

	No. of countries of service	Approx. number of missionaries	Year of founding or early Franson influence
1. Norwegian Mission Covenant ("Lammers" Free Churches–1856) Oslo, Norway	3	30	1884
2. Evangelical Free Church of America Minneapolis, Minnesota USA	10	217	1884
3. Swedish Holiness Union Kumla, Sweden	9	94	1887
4. Danish Mission Covenant Odense, Denmark	3	7	1888
5. The Mission Covenant in Finland Helsingfors, Finland			1888
6. The Free Church of Finland (Finnish Alliance Mission–1895) Helsinki, Finland	14	30	1888

7.	German Alliance Mission (Foreign missions arm of German Evangelical Free Church) Dietzhölztal, West Germany	5	47	1889
8.	Swiss Alliance Mission Winterthur, Switzerland	4	61	1889
9.	The Evangelical Alliance Mission Wheaton, Illinois USA	24	997	1890
10.	Evangelical East Asia Mission (merger of Swedish Mongol Mission–1897 and Swedish Mission in China–1887) Stockholm, Sweden	1	7	1897
11.	Marburg Mission (Foreign missions arm of German Fellowship Deaconry Union) Marburg, West Germany	4	70	1899
12.	Swedish Alliance Mission (Jönköping Association for Home and Foreign Missions–1853) Jönköping, Sweden	17	71	1900
13.	Norwegian Missionary Alliance Oslo, Norway	6	45	1901
14.	Armenian Spiritual Brotherhood			1906

Appendix II

Partial report on the mission field church fellowships arisen around the churches founded through the pioneer "Franson missionaries" before 1910, as reported in the Jönköping Consultation May 27-30, 1981.

Through the Swedish Holiness Union

As of 1950, thirteen churches in North China, 3,000 + members. Ten of the 13 churches were planted between 1895 and 1910.

Through the Swedish Alliance Mission

a. As of 1950, twelve churches and 30 branches in Shansi and Suiyuan Provinces of China, total membership 3,300. Suiyuan Bible Institute had 38 students in 1950.

b. In 1980, sixteen churches in Dhulia-Nandurbar area of Maharashtra State, India, membership 2,825. Four of these churches were planted before 1910.

c. In 1980, 13,000 communicants in South Africa.

Through the Free Church of Finland

In 1980, thirty-one congregations and preaching points in Darjeeling area of India bordering Bhutan, Sikkim, and Nepal. Five churches date from before 1910.

Through The Evangelical Alliance Mission

a. In 1949, Shensi-Kansu Alliance Church Association in China (founded in 1932) had over 100 churches and more than 15,000 baptized members. Twenty churches were opened before 1905. As is true of all churches in China, any tie with overseas organizations was cut in the 1950s. In 1980 news of renewed and expanded church activity was received.

b. In 1980 Japan Evangelical Alliance Church (Domei) reported over 100 member churches with 5,749 members. Four of these churches antedate 1908. Churches of Swiss Alliance Mission and Swedish Alliance Mission are included in the number.

c. In 1980 seventy-five churches in Nasik District, Maharashtra, India were reported. One church was planted in 1906.

d. In 1980 "OVICE" the Organization of Venezuela Evangelical Churches had over 140 member churches and preaching points.

   e. Evangelical churches in South Africa and Swaziland were not reported. Many date back to the 1895-1908 period.

Through the German Alliance Mission and the Swiss Alliance Mission

   As of 1948, 13 churches and 72 branches in Chekiang, and Kiangsi provinces of China reported 2,453 members. Ten of these churches were founded between 1891 and 1906.

Note: This tabulation touches only on the churches which are a direct outgrowth of the ministry of Franson-related missions which began *during the lifetime of the founder*. Omitted are statistics of the extensive later church planting and growth.

Appendix III

The Jönköping Consultation of Franson Founded or Influenced Organizations, Jönköping, Sweden, May 27-30, 1981.

For the first time in the nearly one century since Franson's ministry began exerting a significant influence on the founding, development, and work of the fourteen organizations listed in Appendix I, an effort was made to bring representatives of these organizations together to share information and to establish lines of communication. The Swedish Alliance Mission kindly invited representatives to meet at the Kortebo Bible School facility near Jönköping. To this invitation there was response by all fourteen organizations, with eleven groups sending a total of 35 delegates.

Each organization reported quite fully on its principles of work and the extent of its ministry. Though many of the missions had worked in widely separated areas, there was remarkable similarity of emphasis and very clear cut faithfulness to the evangelical position.

By unanimous vote, the following statement was adopted:

WHEREAS:

The Lord of the Harvest raised up evangelist and world missionary, Fredrik Franson, to labor with abundant fruitfulness for a period of over thirty years until his early home call in 1908, and,

WHEREAS:

His God-directed vision and ministry brought to the attention of the Christian public significant scriptural principles regarding the work of evangelism, the nurture of believers, the polity of the church, and the expectation of Christ's early return, and in that light, of the urgency of the worldwide missionary task, and,

WHEREAS:

The evangelical mission organizations and church fellowships listed herewith recognize Franson either as founder or as one whose influence directly affected the course of their ministries, and,

WHEREAS:

The vital nature of Franson's scriptural principles has been demonstrated in the strong church fellowships and congregations established in scores of countries around the world, and,

WHEREAS:

The present urgent spiritual need of the world with its greatly expanded ripening harvest fields continues greater than when our organizations were founded, and,

WHEREAS:

Our organizations are deeply grateful to God for the common evangelical heritage which is ours;

BE IT RESOLVED:

That we, as individuals meeting in consultation at Jönköping, Sweden, May 27-30, 1981, dedicate ourselves anew to our Lord Jesus Christ, with an earnest desire that the Holy Spirit may use us as His instrument in winning the lost for Christ, building His church, and hastening His return.

That we acknowledge with gratitude the work of basic research on the ministry of Fredrik Franson done by Edvard Torjesen of The Evangelical Alliance Mission and the graciousness of The Swedish Alliance Mission in making possible this consultation.

That our organizations gather and preserve the records of the principles of the outstanding ministry of Franson which gave rise to or influenced our work.

That we seek to publish more widely than before the scriptural principles that were significant in Franson's ministry and in the initiation of our respective works.

That we keep open channels of communication among our organizations by:

a) exchanging our periodicals and other publications.

b) periodic consultations.

c) cooperation where such will enchance our ministries.

That we continue to consider as central in our ministry evangelism leading to the planting and growth of spiritual churches of the New Testament pattern.

That we rejoice in the spiritual maturity of many of the national churches which are taking full responsibility for missionary extension in their own areas and that we strongly encourage them in developing effective foreign mission ministries on their own or in cooperation with their founding missions.

That we recognize that human resolve and endeavor are no substitutes for the gracious working of the Spirit of God in and through every person associated with these ministries, and thus we look to His empowering and leading.

Appendix IV

The Doctrine of the Church
in the Life and Work of Fredrik Franson

Fredrik Franson's influence as a world evangelist and organizer of foreign missions is well known. However, Franson was also a strong promoter of home missions. He was a catalyst in the emergence of the Fellowship of Christians for Joint Mission Work, now the Evangelical Free Church of America; the Mission Covenant of Norway; the Swedish Holiness Union and the Swedish Alliance Mission in Sweden; the Alliance Society at Barmen in western Germany; and the Fellowship Deaconry at Borken, West Prussia, now the Marburg Mission in western Germany. All of this indicates a man with both tremendous cross-cultural facility and a commanding and viable doctrine of the church.

The Setting in Sweden

Fredrik Franson was a true child of the nineteenth-century Swedish-American spiritual awakening.[1] The context of that awakening was a church whose structure and polity had been set in accordance with the terms of the Peace of Augsburg (1555) as modified by the Peace of Westphalia (1648), which was the pattern of all the churches of northern Europe at that time. Receiving the sacraments (baptism and the Lord's supper) and adhering to pure doctrine (whether Augsburg, Belgic, or Helvetic Confessions or the Thirty-nine Articles) had become the main marks of being a Christian. This produced what has been called the Century of Orthodoxy.

The first awakening surges in that situation came to a head in Germany with Philip Spener's emphasis on "living faith" and the subsequent Moravian dispersion. These then influenced the development of Methodism and the religious society movement in England, and the so-called "Luther readerism" in Sweden. Each of these in turn influenced young Carl Olof Rosenius in Sweden, who, during the 1830s–1860s, established as the heart of evangelical theology the concept of the believer's new life in Christ as

[1] See the author's *Fredrik Franson and Church Development on the Swedish-American Frontier*, TS at TEAM, Wheaton, IL. All citations and quotations in this present article are taken from that work.

reflected in the Scriptures alone.[2]

This theology provided the unifying drive of the Swedish-American spiritual awakening. It forced through a new understanding of the church on earth as being composed of believers only—people who had been born again through a living faith in Jesus Christ in accordance with God's Word alone. This led to the development of the Lord's supper societies and missionary associations for believers only that functioned independently of the Swedish state church but remained within its sphere. This, then, was the direction of the spiritual awakening in Sweden when Fredrik Franson emigrated to the United States in 1896 at the age of 17.

The Setting Among the Swedish Immigrants in America

By the time Franson arrived, four denominational groups had already emerged among the Swedish churches in America: The Methodists, the Baptists, the General Lutheran Synod of Northern Illinois, and the Scandinavian Lutheran Augustana Synod. In 1873 the awakening people among the Swedish Lutherans set up their own synod, the Mission Synod, and, in 1874, the Synod of Ansgar. So a total of four Lutheran synods had now been developed among the Swedish-American revivalists. This became a real offense to many of them, because at heart they were really committed to Carl Rosenius's theology and perceived themselves as one in Christ. This was also the case with a good number of the Baptists.

Fredrik Franson, D. L. Moody, and Interchurch Evangelism

Fredrik Franson was converted to Christ in 1872. Two years later he was baptized. He became very active in the Baptist churches, and in 1875 he was elected Secretary of the Swedish Baptist Conference of Western Iowa, Nebraska, and Dakota. That fall, however, when D. L. Moody returned from England and began his American campaigns—in Brooklyn, Philadelphia, Manhattan, and so on, ending with the Chicago campaign of October 1876 to January

---

[2] For a present-day English sampling of Rosenius' writings, see *Rosenius' Daily Meditations*, trans. J. Elmer Dahlgren, rev. Royal F. Peterson (Minneapolis: Lutheran Colportage Service, 1973).

1877—Fredrik Franson disappeared from the Baptist scene in Nebraska. At some point he had begun to study Moody's evangelistic methods and interchurch emphasis, and in February 1877 Franson launched out on his own evangelistic mission, adopting many of D. L. Moody's methods and principles.

For the next two and a half years Fredrik Franson worked largely in Iowa and Minnesota—in both churched and unchurched settlements—among Baptists and Methodists, as well as among the Augustana Lutherans and churches of the Mission Synod and Synod of Ansgar. The Augustana Lutherans opposed him, but several Baptist churches grew significantly as a result of his work. In other settlements, his work contributed to the development of Mission Synod and Synod of Ansgar churches some years later.

The Problem of the Intensifying Divisive Denominationalism

During this period Franson became thoroughly familiar with the factional denominationalism—Methodists, Baptists, and the three Lutheran synods—that kept fragmenting the essential oneness in Christ which the awakening people perceived among themselves in their small frontier settlements. In order to keep his channels open to all of these groups, Franson joined, in August 1878, the only independent and interdenominational church then existing in America—The Moody Church in Chicago. Moody Church furnished him with a letter recognizing his evangelistic work and commending him "to the Lord and to the Lord's people wherever his labors call him."

The developments unfolding at the time show that Fredrik Franson was gauging the situation among the frontier revivalists correctly. The inherent sense of oneness among these people was so strong that at the Synod of Ansgar's May 1878 annual meeting the motion had prevailed to explore the possibility of uniting with the Mission Synod. The Mission Synod responded at its May 1879 annual meeting by appointing three delegates to meet in a joint committee with three Synod of Ansgar delegates "to draw up a plan by which the two synods could possibly be united." Before the close of that annual meeting, this committee was able to draw up and unanimously recommend such a plan. However, the leadership of the Mission Synod had no desire for such a union, and in the end the plan was tabled.

Fredrik Franson had not yet reached his twenty-seventh birthday at this time. He was probably working somewhere in Minnesota with his friend J. F. Fredrickson of St. Paul. However, the turmoil among the awakening people, brought about because of the divisive denominationalism of their churches, kept troubling him. He was forced to begin thinking about how they could find a way out of their predicament that would be both scripturally and culturally pertinent. It was in this context that Fredrik Franson wrote his first published article, "A Contribution to the Solution of the Complicated Denominational and Local Church Question." The article was published May 23, 1879—just one week before that fateful annual meeting of the Mission Synod.

Fredrik Franson's Basic Perspective on Interchurch Relationships

In this article Fredrik Franson deals with the problems of and cure for factions and factionalism, both *within* and *between* local churches. He also suggests "a good way to take" in the future once the problem has been dealt with. He establishes his basic perspective using the following scriptural analogy:

> Much damage was done to the church in Corinth when one member said, "I follow Apollos," another, "I follow Paul," etc. But the damage would have been far more terrible if one of these factions had begun to check around in other churches—in the churches of Rome, Thessalonica, and Berea, for instance, or in one of the churches of Asia Minor—to see if there might not be some like-minded groups in these churches, and if these groups had then organized themselves into a denomination with Paul as its head, or with Peter or Apollos. *But this did not happen* either in the Corinthian church or in any of the others. That was because they heeded Paul's admonition, and the tendency was suppressed in time.

In Franson's day, however, the situation was no longer the same. As he surveyed the scene, Franson could see groupings of churches "stretching out like tightly-knit corporations from city to city and country to country, each trying in its own best way to gain adherents." He therefore submits five steps as a cure to this malady: (1) See the situation; (2) Acknowledge the disease; (3) Will to get rid of it; (4) Take the cure—"Christ's spirit, the spirit of love, is the best antidote for factionalism;" (5) Find a good way to take from here on out.

In the rest of his article, Franson sets up principles for such a "good way." He finds that the prerequisites have already been established by the precedents recorded in the Acts of the Apostles. He says, "I believe our ideas will get a lot clearer if we keep in mind that during the days of the apostles the whole executive power lay in the hands of the individual local congregation and not in the hands of a denomination, synod, or conference."

Each Church Its Own Synod—Responsible to Cultivate the Gifts and Calling of All its Members for its Needed Leadership and Spiritual Nurture in Accordance with the Scriptures.

How is this executive power described in the Acts of the Apostles? Franson points to Acts 13 where five "prophets and teachers" are named as the leaders of the Antioch church. What is the particular leadership functions these five men carried out? They were prophets and teachers. For a definition of the prophetic ministry, Franson draws on Paul's statement in I Cor. 14:3, "Everyone who prophesies speaks to men for their *strengthening, encouragement, and comfort.*" Then he adds:

> It is quite clear that it was these five brothers who identified the two among them as having been chosen by the Holy Spirit to go out and preach the gospel and, after that, they proceeded to ordain them in the way described. These prophets and teachers were all found within this one single local congregation—just as today you also often find within one single local congregation those who can speak to the church for its strengthening, encouragement, and comfort. We also note how these men did what they did without having to send Paul and Barnabas either hither or yon to get ordination.

Franson then points to the Ephesus church, where the leaders are called "overseers" or "elders" (Acts 20:17,28). We must recognize, nevertheless, he says, that these leaders were appointed "through the leadership of the Holy

Spirit" no less than those "prophets and teachers" in the Antioch church. Similarly, the Holy Spirit's leadership must also be recognized in such expressions as "when the body of elders laid their hands on you" in I Tim. 4:14.

As Franson applies these scriptural precedents to the situation existing in the Swedish Lutheran revival churches in America, he writes:

> It is not difficult to see that if we would keep in mind these precedents, the best way to solve the question about the synods would be for each congregation to act as its own synod. The word "synod" does not occur in the Bible; neither—unless I am mistaken—does the word "conference" with reference to God's church. On the other hand, the Acts of the Apostles does record several *consultations* with the local Jerusalem church. These consultations are a good pattern then, as are also the procedure by which the Jerusalem church communicated the findings of these consultations to the other churches and the response of these churches to those findings (see Acts 15:22-29).

Each Church One With All of Christ's Other Churches— Expressed Through Mutual Interchurch Evangelism and Other Mutually Acceptable Interchurch Projects—and Their Common Hope in Christ in Accordance with the Scriptures.

From here Franson goes on to the question of the churches' relationship to each other. He asks, "Did not the churches then stand in any kind of outward relationship to each other?" He answers:

> As far as I have been able to find out, only through the itinerant evangelists or missionaries. These individuals transmitted the funds that had come in—one for this purpose, another for that. They also stimulated the churches "to wholesome thinking" by bringing to the minds of the people "the words spoken in the past by the holy prophets and the command given by our Lord and Savior through your apostles" (II Peter 3:1,2) which we also have in our Bibles today—complete and not in need of new resolutions of any kind.

These, then, were the two main points which Franson held out as prerequisites for the "good way to take" in getting rid of and staying away from divisive denominationalism: (1) let each local church function as its own synod, fully responding to God's Word and the Holy Spirit's leadership in developing its own needed leadership and spiritual nurture, and (2) let each local church relate itself responsibly both to the world around it and to all of Christ's other churches here on earth in accordance with the Word of God and the leadership of the Holy Spirit. He concludes: "When Jesus comes, he will not be looking for more than one bride. Nor will he be looking for a divided bride. When Jesus comes, all whom he then takes up will be those who are all one in him!"

The Application of This Prescription in Utah

The young Fredrik Franson soon had an unexpected opportunity to apply these prerequisites to three completely new situations in which both he and the principles were put to the test. He had planned to leave for an evangelistic mission in Sweden, but now the Lord called him to go to Utah instead. Here God placed him in the first revival surges ever recorded in the history of Protestant work in Utah. In one town thirty persons confessed Christ, in another, sixteen.

To shepherd these new converts, a number of them directly from Mormonism, Franson worked with the local Presbyterian missionary to discover to whom among these people had been granted gifts of leadership. Then these two godly servants drew up a church covenant designed to serve as a reminder to the new converts of their responsibilities to each other in the Lord. They also organized two Presbyterian churches among them—one with two elders and two deacons, the other with one elder. This all happened less than a year after Franson had written the article on "a good way to take."

The Application in Denver

After this, Fredrik Franson was led to stop in Colorado, where he began to witness among Swedes in the scattered mining communities of the Rockies, and also among the five hundred or so Swedes in Denver.

Here, also, God granted an awakening, and on July 26, 1880, the Scandinavian Church of Denver was organized

with fifteen charter members. Three elders and two deaconesses were elected. One of the elders, a shoemaker recently arrived from Brooklyn, New York, was selected to
serve as pastor. The next day they recorded the incorporation of this new church in the office of the county clerk. In
that record they inserted the following statement:

> This body of believers desires to be known only as Chris-
> tians, without reference to any denomination, yet regarding
> all who hold and preach the truth contained in our articles
> of faith as equally belonging to the same Head, and is
> thereby free to cooperate and unite with such people in car-
> rying out the work of our common Master.

That statement, with its affirmation of desire to stay
away from divisive denominationalism and to instead develop solidarity with all those "equally belonging to the same
head," comes from the original "Principles of Organization"
of The Moody Church adopted in 1864.[3] Franson, now a
member of The Moody Church, clearly feels that its principles of organization will set this new Scandinavian Church
of Denver on a good course. Moreover, some three months
later he takes special pains to make the doctrinal position of
this new church absolutely clear. He writes:

> These friends will gladly receive visits from any brother
> who believes in and serves Jesus. They desire to be one with
> all who are the brothers and sisters of Jesus, recognizing
> that together with them they make up one and the same
> body. They consider that variant concepts about points not
> vital to the life in Christ ought not to hinder in any way
> brotherly love or the extension of full brotherly fellowship.
> Consequently, they have left to each believer individually
> such questions as, for instance, the various doctrines about
> the mode, time, and meaning of baptism, so that on these
> questions each believer may believe and act in accordance
> with his own best understanding of the Word of God without
> having to feel even the slightest strangeness from his fellow
> believers in the flock.

We see, then, that Fredrik Franson's concern is not merely to form a church composed of all those—and only those—
in its community who have life in Christ. Nor is he concerned
merely to form a church that will cultivate the gifts of every

---

[3] See "Mr. Moody's Church," in W. H. Daniels, *D. L. Moody and His Work* (Hart-
ford: American Publishing, 1876), esp. 108-112.

member so that it may adequately develop its own leadership and spiritual nurture. Also, he is not merely concerned to form a church whose hope in Christ will condition its outlook on and mission in the world in accordance with the Scriptures. What he is really trying to do is form a church that will respond to all that is in the Scriptures—and only to that which is in the Scriptures—as the truth in Christ, and will aim to express in its structure and polity the simultaneous *oneness* and *freedom* in Christ of all believers in accordance with this truth. Such a church must be *simply* evangelical and free.

Of course, such a church is also its own synod. But for a church to be without denominational responsibility does not make its burden of responsibility any less. In fact, that local church now must assume its *scriptural responsibility* to relate itself fully to its members, to the world around it, and to all of Christ's other churches on earth *as the local churches in the New Testament did.* That is the genius of what Fredrik Franson was trying to accomplish in the founding of the Scandinavian Church of Denver.

Did the 28-year-old Franson really know what the implications would be if a local church were to assume this scriptural responsibility? Here we must do a little reading between the lines. We do not know that Fredrik Franson ever received any further formal education, theological or otherwise, after he had to drop out of high school in Sweden at the end of his freshman year when he was sixteen. However, ever since his conversion at age twenty, Franson had submitted himself to a rigorous and serious personal study of the Bible. He also reflects a considerable knowledge of other literature, especially on theological, social, and historical issues. He understood human nature and was a perceptive observer of social movements. His quick understanding of and accommodation to the situation in Utah is a good illustration of this. But if there is any doubt as to whether Franson really understood the implications of a local church's assuming the full scriptural responsibility he advocated, his response to the situation he met in Nebraska should dispel those doubts once and for all.

**The Application in Phelps and
Kearney Counties, Nebraska**

Before the end of November 1880—less than two months
after he had left Denver—Fredrik Franson had already
been used of God in an awakening in Phelps and Kearney
counties, Nebraska, through which four new churches were
developed.

The revival itself began through a Bible study conference
on the Lord's return. Then it turned into a serious study of
the biblical pattern of the local church, a question some of
the local believers had been concerned about for some time.

Fortunately, two primary sources from this revival still
exist. One is the official report of Leander Hallgren, the secretary of the original Bible study conference. The other is an
expanded rewrite by Fredrik Franson himself of a message
he had given on "The Biblical Pattern of the Local Church."
This rewrite takes up fourteen full-size newspaper pages. I
shall try to bring out some of the more salient points of both
sources.

The Composition of the Local Church

Franson deals at length with the composition of the local
church. He says, "Clearly such a church is composed of
spiritually alive persons," people who, "like living stones,
are built into a spiritual house to be a holy priesthood" (I
Peter 2:5). As such they need to know "how people ought to
conduct themselves in God's household, which is the church
of the living God" (I Tim. 3:15). The church is, then, likened
to a building, and its members to the stones of which it is
built.

What are the prerequisites for a stone to go into that
building? Franson points out, first of all, that each stone
must be cut so that one or more of its surfaces will fit the
corresponding surfaces on the stones to be placed next to it.
There can be no misfitting—no joining together of a cut and
an uncut stone, of a converted and an unconverted person—
or the house will soon crack, perhaps even collapse. The
complete fit, then, of the two adjoining surfaces of all the
stones is an absolute necessity.

But this is not enough. A third set of surfaces is also important—the surface of each stone that is part of the out-

side facing of the building. Franson puts it this way:

> During the organization of the church in Phelps, one brother emphasized that it is not enough that someone who applies for admission to the church only has spiritual life. His *manner* of life also must be above reproach. The world sees only the outside facing of God's house. If there is any stone in that facing whose surface has not been cut to fit, then the world notices that one stone before all the others. There are many Christians about whom one cannot deny that they have life, but who are still not fit to be taken into the local church because of carelessness in their daily dealings with other people. . . . If we are responsive to God's Spirit in the admission of members, then such a person will not dare to join God's people without first having confessed his sins—unless he wants to make himself a complete hypocrite, whom God alone will finally judge.

The stones have a fourth set of surfaces as well—the surface on each stone that makes up the inside facing of the building. "As long as we are in this life," says Franson, "this inside surface of our lives will have some pretty rough spots in it; but, praise God, He is the only one who ever sees it. Let me say this: no Christian will ever need to be afraid of living a life completely separated to the Lord because he might not then have any more need to pray the fifth petition in the Lord's prayer. No, my brother and sister, you still will have need to ask *God* for the forgiveness of your sins—even if all the world and all God's children together should not be able to find one single fault with you."

Leander Hallgren's Report

With such a standard, how did the people in these young settlers' communities on the prairie go about receiving members into the new churches they were establishing?

Leander Hallgren tells us that when the vote was called on whether or not to set up a church on the biblical pattern, one man dissented, because he was afraid "that many who do not live fully for Jesus might actually favor the idea of local church freedom and, therefore, it might even be possible that some unsaved people would try to get involved." The people readily acknowledged the danger of this and "adopted the greatest care in the admission of members into the free local church."

Their first step was to select "six brothers who had the
general confidence of all." These six then nominated six
others "whom the whole flock of those who confessed
themselves as Christians voted on." Then these twelve nominated six others, and these too were voted on in the same
way, making a total of eighteen who had been selected by
this method. These eighteen were the charter members of
the church, "for after that no one else was permitted to
vote."

The eighteen charter members then selected six persons
from among themselves to serve as a membership committee. In the first round, this membership committee nominated six more from among the confessing believers, whom
all the charter members then voted on and received into the
congregation. Then others were nominated and similarly
received by the now-growing congregation, until its membership reached 32. At this point the congregation elected three
elders and three deacons, who, together with the trustees
and the clerk, "were to make up the standing committee on
the admission and dismissal of members, acting in the name
of the church and according to its charge." Afterwards,
when "it became clear that to preach and to testify about
Jesus is the responsibility of all God's children, each according to his gift," the church also decided to elect four
deaconesses. In this way, by the time Hallgren wrote his
report at the beginning of December, the church already
had seventy members.

Hallgren's report concentrates mainly on the church at
Phelps Centre, but he also reports on the development of the
churches at Keene and Westmark. In each place there were
different features that struck him. In Keene, for instance,
"it was a joy to see the flock of these children, who before
had belonged to five separate communions, now give to each
other their hands as brothers and sisters in one family." At
Westmark the people followed the same procedure in admit-
ting members as at Phelps Centre, but here they also responded to God's call to set aside one of their brothers to do
the work of an evangelist. For four years that man served as
the pastor of this church, and then he moved out into an itinerant ministry.

The Church's Responsibility to Its Members

Franson saw the local church as being responsible to its members in at least three distinct areas: (1) involving every member meaningfully in the general work of the church; (2) involving every member meaningfully in the meetings of the church; and (3) acknowledging and cultivating God's gifts to the church as distributed among all of its members. He says:

The purpose of the local church is that *all* be workers. I like old Mr. Wesley's slogan: "All at it and always at it!" May no one join a local church with the idea that now he has fulfilled his obligation. Joining a church is only the *acknowledgment* that now I intend to fulfill my obligation.

Sometimes I am almost afraid to try to help organize a new church. For if those who join do not get the right concept of the purpose of the local church, then all the to-do becomes nothing more than to *make camp.* . . .

If every child of God has been given at least one gift, then it becomes very important for us not only to know which gift each member has been given, but also that we fan that gift into flame. That gift can be used not only in the general meetings of the church, but also on a thousand different occasions between the meetings.

Franson then gives a detailed explanation of the church's responsibility in each of these three areas, and he concludes: "When a church rigorously seeks to cultivate God's gift to its every member and then uses every member both in its general work and in its public meetings in accordance with these gifts, then that which is the church's goal—the strengthening of God's children and the salvation of the lost—is best achieved."

The Distribution of Members' Functions in the Local Church

Franson describes the minimum organization of a local church as "a free and independent local congregation in which there is structure and polity." Such a church has an orderly distribution of functions among its various members. Some functions clearly apply to the *general membership* as a whole; other functions apply only to the *leadership*. For instance, I Cor. 14:31 asserts explicitly, "You can all prophesy in turn so that everyone may be instructed and encouraged." Franson concludes:

All may thus speak to strengthen, encourage, and comfort [cf. I Cor 14:3]; and *all* may also be taught and comforted from such speaking. In other words, *all* may be preachers; and *all* may be listeners. But the record shows that there were also certain especially selected persons—those with the nobler gifts in this one or some other area—who were called "the elders"; and in every congregation these numbered *more than one*. . . . See Acts 13:1; 14:23; 51:2,4,6,22, 23; 20:17; 20:28-30 and Phil. 1:1. . . . From these passages we see that in no less than eight congregations—Antioch, Derbe, Lystra, Iconium, Antioch of Pisidia, Ephesus, Jerusalem, and Philippi—there were *several elders* in each of them.

The Nobler Gifts

Concerning the elders Franson says:

These elders, like all God's children in general, have different gifts—such as those we find described in Eph. 4:11 and I Cor. 12:28. . . . For instance, in addition to the apostles, who also counted themselves as among the elders. . . we note in particular *prophets, evangelists, pastors,* and *teachers.* That these gifts are present in every congregation, if only they are drawn out and cultivated, we can readily see even today whenever and wherever the Spirit of God is working. We see many at such times who have the gift to shepherd or pastor—often quite unobtrusively—those who are newly converted. . . . The same is also true with regard to the teaching ministry.

To Franson it is extremely important that these gifts be used. He says, "There is one thing I have noticed: when God's children will not make use of the gifts God has given them for his praise, then the devil will get hold of those gifts." He also notes that there is a significant distribution even among these nobler gifts. For instance:

Those church members selected for the office of elder seem to have been those to whom the Holy Spirit had committed the noblest gifts. However, it was not required that all of these elders be public speakers. For instance, Paul indicates in I Tim. 5:17 that some elders are engaged in tasks other than preaching and teaching. . . . They had been given other gifts—for instance, the gift of administration—that qualified them for inclusion on the elders' roll.

Franson finds that these nobler gifts fall into three

categories: elders, deacons, and evangelists. The elders and deacons are the *administrative* officers of the church. The evangelists are its *extension* officers. For the validity of the distinction between the elders and the deacons, Franson refers to Phil. 1:1 and, particularly, I Tim. 3, "where the duties of both the elders and the deacons are set forth."

The Evangelists—the Church's Extension Officers

Fredrik Franson states his basic perspective concerning the evangelist's gift as follows:

> In each local church there are those who have that special gift—the evangelist's gift—the gift to communicate with those still unconverted. . . . When it is noticed that someone in the church has that gift, then it becomes important that that person be encouraged in every possible way both to deal with souls privately and to witness to them publicly. And if that person continues to let God's Spirit lead him, he should be encouraged also to go out with an older brother to do similar witnessing in other places. . . . Many churches have experienced brothers who well could go out like that and witness about Jesus.

Franson deals at considerable length with the evangelist's function as an extension officer of the local church. He isolates three areas in particular for consideration: (1) The responsibilities of the local believers in the evangelist's target area; (2) the responsibilities of the evangelist himself in the target area; and (3) the continuing transmission of the evangelist's commission.

The Responsibilities of the Local Believers in the Evangelist's Target Area

Significantly, Franson considers the local believers' own responsibilities in the target area first, before he considers the evangelist's responsibilities there. To him it was absolutely essential that all local believers become significantly involved in the evangelist's mission in the target area, that this involvement be respected by both the evangelist and the local believers as an *essential goal* of that mission, and that both they and he work for it rigorously and do nothing to hinder it. Franson states his basic proposition as follows:

> God's children in each locality are the preachers who should speak for the mutual strengthening of one another

and also preach to the unsaved there. God seems to have a rule that as long as an evangelist can work with good fruit *among the unsaved* in a locality, he ought to remain there, and so far all is well—even if he has to have four or five meetings a day—since God's Spirit is with him. But after that, God's will seems to be that the evangelist "must preach the good news about the kingdom of God in the other towns also," and when this is done, God's children still seem to fare just as well—even though they are left by themselves to build each other up through those gifts which only exist within the church. Then after some time, perhaps God's Spirit may again have moved in such a way that more people are under conviction; and then God will—in answer to the prayers of his children there—save those people, either without any visiting evangelist, or by sending back the same one who left earlier, or even someone else.

The Responsibilities of the Evangelist Himself in His Target Area

When Franson turns to the evangelist's own responsibilities in his target area, his insistent advice is that, both for his own sake, as well as for the sake of the local church, the evangelist should resist the temptation to settle down and "preach to God's children" in that area. He says:

An evangelist who settles down to do the work of a resident pastor first hurts *himself*, since he could do three times as much work and have ten times as happy a life if he would dedicate himself to "do the work of an evangelist"; and then he also hurts *the people*, since he will rob them, in most cases, of their own rightful opportunity to use their own gifts. We have seen some exceptions to this rule, as, for instance, when there is a large field among the unsaved in the area in which the evangelist has settled, and his work then becomes more that of an evangelist to the unsaved, rather than a preacher to God's children. In such cases, the evangelist sees his work as being not so much to preach as with a gentle hand merely to lead the meetings—or, in other words, sees his work as *putting God's people to work*.

Franson then takes up a number of illustrations of this policy, both from its many precedents in the Scriptures, as well as from the way God's blessings have rested on a number of evangelists and evangelistic movements of his own day following this policy.

The Continuing Transmission
of the Evangelist's Commission

To Fredrik Franson the local church's evangelism program did not consist merely of a series of spot campaigns,
but of a continuous, integrated, and integrating long-range
campaign. He says, "The closer we get to the biblical way of
doing missionary work, the better.... What the apostolic
local churches occupied themselves with was not—as is the
case with so many local churches in our day—to call pastors. It was to send out evangelists, and to do this directly in
response to the Holy Spirit's call and leadership as to where
they should go." He sees two essential stages in this program. The first stage is what happened when Paul and Barnabas were commissioned by the rest of the elders in the
Antioch church. What particular meaning did that event
have? Franson answers:

It was simply this, that the elders in Antioch had gotten it
clear that the gospel ought to be preached in other places
and that they, therefore, *separated from* among *themselves*
those whom the Lord already had so called and separated.
This the Holy Spirit had already revealed to them. Through
the laying of hands on Paul and Barnabas, the rest of the
elders, therefore, *joined together in prayer to God for these
two colleagues of theirs* that his Spirit might go with them on
their missionary trip. This was a setting apart carried out in
the place from which the evangelists were sent out. There is
no mention of any call *from* the places to which they were going. The great darkness in which the self-righteous Jews and
the pagan Gentiles were living was call enough for them.
Moreover, if in some of the places there should happen to be
Christians, and these should have fallen into a spiritual
slumber, then I believe that their precarious condition would
have been a strong enough call for anyone with a flaming
love for Jesus.

This is the starting point of the evangelist's commission in
the local church. But how is that commission transmitted on-
ward? Through a repetition of the Antioch precedent in
each place where God has granted fruit through the evangelist's message. Here is how Franson described that second
stage:

The simple apostolic procedure in the evangelistic extension of the church was that in each area when the evangelist

was organizing a local church, he would set apart elders
through the laying on of hands. Later, when the evangelist's
gift in turn had developed among some of these elders, these
would be set apart by the remaining elders in that church
and sent out on their evangelistic mission. These evangelists
would then in turn lay hands on the elders in other new congregations they were organizing—and so on continually.
This is the way, for instance, in which Timothy was set apart
through the laying on of the hands of the elders (I Tim. 4:14),
and then he in turn laid his hands on others (I Tim. 5:22).

In connection with the setting apart of evangelists for this
extension work of the local church, Franson also discusses
the issuing of licenses or letters of recommendation. He
says, "We recognize, of course, that it is the Holy Spirit who
in the first place gives license or authority to preach. Nevertheless, it is both well and necessary that an evangelist who
goes out to witness about the Lord has the recommendation
of some local church that he is a brother in Christ as well as
a worker in the vineyard. We find, for instance, that the
apostles wrote such letters—some for the purpose of recom-
mending (as in Col. 4:7-9, Rom. 16:1,2, and III John 5-8), and
others for the purpose of warning (as in II Tim. 2:17, 4:15,
and III John 9,10).

Before leaving this point, Franson writes:

> The laying on of hands accompanied by the prayers to God
> of his children is something that brings a great blessing with
> it. As I took part in calling down God's blessing on the elders
> in the Phelps church, I could not help but wish—as a brother
> in Minnesota had said it once—"Surely, this is something I
> need every time I go to preach." Therefore, even though
> twice before I have been set apart through the laying on of
> hands by God's children, I could not keep from asking now
> that these elders set me apart for the third time. They did
> this when I was about to leave, and the elders together with
> the whole congregation of God's children joined together in
> prayer for me that God's blessing might rest on me wherever
> he might lead me.

The Interchurch Relationships of the Local Church

Franson now moves on to consider the interchurch relationships of the local church. He states his basic perspective
as follows:

All God's children in all localities throughout the world have a natural oneness with one another in the bonds of love and peace because they are all the children of the same *Father*, they all make up the *Bride of Christ*, have the *same Holy Spirit*, the *same Word* to lead them, and they are all aiming for the *same heaven*. As such, they are responsive to each other, sense their participation with one another, and when the need arises, seek in all respects to help each other *voluntarily* as they did in the days of the apostles (Acts 11:29). But, in addition, they are also—and that as a matter of course—firmly committed to each other in their *common task for the Lord*...because of which they *rejoice together* in each other's victories...and *intercede together* concerning each other's burdens.

Nevertheless, Franson makes it clear that as to the local churches' entering into a *structured interchurch relationship* to each other, this is "something about which the Bible says nothing." He says:

The Bible speaks in explicit detail about many facets of the relationship between God's children on the local level. For instance, there are instructions about those who comprise the local congregations, including information on the listing and numbering of believers in a locality, their congregational officers, the selection, qualification, and job descriptions of such officers, how to deal with improper behavior—among the members as well as among the officers of the congregation—and how the meetings and evangelistic outreach of the congregations are to be carried out, etc. But in all these instructions there is not one single word about synods or denominational conferences, as, for instance, some resolution, or the meetings and officers of such a synod, or the selection, qualifications, and duties of such interchurch officers, or the regulations by which they carry out their interchurch business, etc. It seems to me then that this ought to be decisive in the matter.

As Franson sums up these findings, he comes back to the point he had made the year before in his May 1879 article: "A good deal of heartache, concern, unrest, and time consumed, as well as responsibilities involved in the maintenance of a synod, can be avoided if each congregation would stay as its own synod." However, he adds: "All those who join themselves together in independent local churches must be careful to show—by their deeds as well as by their fruits—that they also are one with all God's children." He concludes with the following observations:

> Sometimes I have thought that since our Lord's return seems to be so very near, perhaps this is not the appropriate time to speak up on the structuring of the local church. But when we stop to think that both holding forth the doctrine of the Lord's return to God's children and working for the salvation of the unconverted world are exactly the purposes for which the church on earth exists and is being brought into being, then it becomes quite clear that in every locality God's children ought to band themselves together as closely as possible—so that they may utilize with greater zeal the few days left them to serve the Lord efficiently.

This was the doctrine of the church that Fredrik Franson sought to reinforce among the awakening people in Nebraska in the fall of 1880. It sought to pattern before them a local church that would relate itself dynamically to all of its members, to the whole world around it, and to all of Christ's other churches on earth *as the churches in the New Testament had done.* It called on this local church to express in its own structure and polity the dynamic relationship between the simultaneous *freedom* and *oneness* in Christ of all believers in accordance with the Scriptures.

Cross-cultural Control Factors

Fredrik Franson had worked out this doctrine of the church in a very significant cross-cultural and interdenominational situation. His own boyhood was spent in the revival milieu of Sweden. As a young settler on the American frontier he became converted, was baptized, and became very active in the Swedish Baptist churches of Nebraska and Iowa. Then he studied D. L. Moody's interdenominational evangelistic campaigns and in his twenty-fifth year, launched out on his own interdenominational evangelistic work. For two and a half years he worked in Iowa and Minnesota, among Baptists, Methodists, and the three Lutheran synods begun among the Swedish settlers there. During this time he joined The Moody Church and wrote the article on "a good way to take." Now he had applied the suggestions in this article to a series of spiritual awakenings through which seven new churches were brought into being in three highly diverse Swedish-American cultural situations: the Utah territory; Denver, Colorado; and Phelps and Kearney counties, Nebraska.

Despite the fact that all seven churches had come into existence through one process, each developed its own original and distinctive form. Nevertheless, as Franson was developing and applying his doctrine of the church in these as well as in many later applications, it is abundantly clear that certain control factors were followed in every situation: (1) theological consistency—not merely with one given confession or statement of faith, but with the full primitive theology of the New Testament churches; (2) efficiency by the local church in carrying out its full scriptural responsibility through its own particular cultural setting; and (3) scriptural church discipline applied rigorously to every member.

To Fredrik Franson a statement of faith—particularly an nonamendable one—which said either *more* or *less* than Scripture explicitly required, was not enough. In its organizational meeting the Keene church had declared that "this church adopts the New Testament as its constitution." Four years later, that same control factor was written into the Boone Declaration by the Fellowship of Christians for Joint Mission Work—now the Evangelical Free Church of America. Faithfulness to *all* that is in the Scriptures, is then the first control factor in applying this doctrine of the church.

Second, commitment to primitive biblical theology made it possible to develop a variety of church forms, in order that the local church might be more efficient in carrying out its full scriptural responsibility whatever its cultural situation. As this doctrine of the church was applied, church forms as varied as the Evangelical Free Church of America, the Mission Covenant of Norway, and the Alliance Society in Barmen, Germany, were developed.

But a third control factor also was applied—the scriptural church discipline of every member. How rigorously this was applied in the Phelps Centre church we have already seen in the reports from Franson and Hallgren. To Franson there could be no church discipline without a properly applied membership procedure. To him this was simply a part of the local church's scriptural responsibility. In Norway, for instance, he chided the inner mission movement for having let people become members of its local organizations by merely "signing up." He urged instead that they adopt "a real admission in accordance with God's Word—and only of real believers." And in the Dutch Reformed Church in South Africa, where he once worked for more than a year at the invitation of Andrew Murray, he found that even though its churches had both converted and unconverted members in them, yet, because the pastors generally acknowledged this and were open to evangelistic work among their own church members, the Lord blessed. In this case, the possibility of practicing church discipline was clearly contingent on the church's acknowledging this state of affairs, and, as Franson points out, "Only where this kind of honesty exists can God's Spirit produce revival."

This doctrine of the church, then, which Fredrik Franson produced when he still was only 28 years old, was based so solidly on primitive biblical theology that it could be applied pertinently to a wide variety of cultural situations—from the pluralistic, cross-cultural situations on the American frontier to the monolithic, state-church dominated situations in northern Europe. It would later be applied in such culturally diverse areas as Africa, India, and China. This doctrine, together with the doctrine of the Lord's return at any time, came to characterize all of Fredrik Franson's work for the next 28 years, until the Lord called him home in 1908.

ABOUT THE AUTHOR

Born in North China of Norwegian missionary parents, the Rev. Edvard Torjesen received his education in China, Norway, Canada, and the United States. During his first term of missionary service, he and his wife, Jenny, also from Norway, worked among the Mongol people, first in Inner Mongolia, then in Hong Kong and Taiwan. In subsequent terms of service the Torjesens' efforts focused on the aboriginal Amis tribespeople of Taiwan. Mr. Torjesen reduced the Amis language to writing.

At present Mr. Torjesen is representating The Evangelical Alliance Mission in North Europe. He works in close cooperation with European evangelical missions and provides pre-missionary career counseling for students in Bible schools and seminaries.